25 SKETCHES ABOUT PROVERBS

For Mum

25 Sketches About Proverbs

DAVID BURT

KINGSWAY PUBLICATIONS
EASTBOURNE

ISBN 0 85476 871 8

Published by
KINGSWAY PUBLICATIONS
Lottbridge Drove, Eastbourne, BN23 6NT, England.
E-mail: books@kingsway.co.uk

Designed and produced for the publishers by
Bookprint Creative Services, P.O. Box 827, BN21 3YJ, England.
Printed in Great Britain.

Contents

Performance and Copyright

The right to perform sketches in this book is included in the price, provided that such performances are made within an amateur context, for example worship or education. Where any charge is made to audiences, permission in writing must be obtained from the author, who can be contacted care of the publisher, and a fee may be payable for the right to do this.

Please note that the text of this book is copyright, and that no part may be copied without permission in writing from the publisher. Where multiple copies of a sketch are required for those playing the parts, it is generally simpler and cheaper to buy extra copies of the book.

Acknowledgements

My thanks to a veritable plethora of family and friends who have been so encouraging and supportive during the writing of this collection. For everyone who has helped me to perform different sketches, and made up read-through audiences, your honest opinions were invaluable.

For hours of hysterical improvisation, my thanks to Tom, and to others who have given me ideas and shared with me their favourite proverbs, many of which I developed into sketches.

A very special mention also goes to Niall, who proves that the biggest inspiration can often come in the smallest (three foot!) packages.

For Soapboxers up and down the country, thanks for your enthusiastic support; especially to Steve, Sarah, Mark and Kev for the unforgettable Dig the Beat experience. (Victor still cannot believe they charge £1.79 for a service station coffee!)

For the hardworking team at Kingsway central my appreciation, particularly to Richard, even though he tries his best to avoid me and has absolutely dreadful taste in music. (Celine Dion, would you credit!)

And finally to trustworthy Dave, the manuscript man, for

all his help, though I reckon in all honesty he only procrastinates on the computer to avoid poopy baby nappies! ... You're all ab fab!

God Bless

Dave

Introduction

It was with truckloads of enthusiasm and a few ready-made ideas that I suggested to Kingsway a book of sketches based around the book of Proverbs. My proposal seemed to contain a whirlpool of sketch material, with wisdom and practical advice for everyone. So, after a small amount of hawking, the book was commissioned.

Although I'd read through Proverbs more than once in the past, I decided that before I put pen to paper, I should spend an extended period of time really studying the book, with the aid of various commentaries. During this period my eyes were truly opened and my brain, well, very nearly exploded! As I began to unpack the book, the incredible depth and profundity of Proverbs gradually dawned on me. Thirty-one chapters, each containing up to 35 verses of erudite couplets, confirmed what I had long suspected. Solomon, Agur and Lemuel each possessed more wisdom in their little fingers than I had in my entire body!

So the exciting task of producing dramatic material to communicate the proverbs, suddenly became a daunting one. How could I hope to encapsulate these teachings in 25 short drama pieces? Not only was there a vast number of these sayings, but each one had such depth that it could speak to different people on a variety of levels. The simple answer, I quickly concluded, was that I could not! Before I even began work I removed the pressure of having to communicate the whole message of this incredible book, and instead set out to identify some key themes and teachings, before attempting to dramatise them in sketch form. In addition to this I decided to include a section giving the reader some ideas on how to work within a group improvising around Proverbs; the reason for this being very simple: if I cannot attain the unrivalled brain power of King Solomon on my own, maybe with all our collected grey matter we can combine to get nearer to these lofty heights! The cynics among you may feel it's rather a rip-off to shell out good money on a book and then have to do half of the work yourself – I prefer to think of it as my solitary moment of marketing genius.

If you fancy having a go on your own, get stuck into the improvisation section of the book and be truly amazed at what you can come up with in a relatively short space of time. For those of you looking for ready-to-use sketches, I hope the themes I have selected from the vast array available prove resourceful in your situation.

You may notice that some sketches appear to offer questions without giving an obvious answer. This is an unusual method in Christian drama. Surely their point should be to hammer home the gospel or whichever biblical truth they are attempting to communicate as clearly as possible? In this next section, before I move on to improvisation ideas, I want to examine the reasons why I have used this style for some of the sketches in this book.

Christian drama: style and substance

In the introduction to my first book, *50 Sketches About Jesus*,

I gave a lengthy defence for using drama to communicate Christian faith and the gospel. Refreshing the parts and emotions other communication forms cannot reach, drama can inform, stimulate and entertain in a unique way. With a few exceptions the sketches I wrote for that first book clearly communicated either the gospel or one of Jesus' teachings, and in effect tied them up with a pretty pink bow. For many of the sketches in this book, however, I have used a different style.

For a piece of Christian drama to work, as with any piece of theatre, certain rules apply. One of these, to put it in its simplest form, is that the piece must have both STYLE and SUBSTANCE. You've heard the saying 'all style and no substance'. If we take this as one warning, and then reverse it, 'all substance and no style', we have two pitfalls to avoid when writing or performing.

Style

Whether you create an individual style of your own, or use an established genre or playwright's style (Shakespearian, Pinteresque, Brechtian, Berkoffian), a piece needs to have a certain *joie de vivre* to work on the stage. This is created with a mix of writing and performing and has the effect of giving the written word life and making it fascinating to watch.

Harold Pinter plays are immediately recognisable by his individual dialogue style: the characters may have a long discussion, often using only a couple of words at a time. Steven Berkoff plays are also easily distinguishable, but for very different reasons. His characters' dialogues are more like verbal explosions – highly descriptive and often written in rhyme similar to iambic pentameter. In performance Berkoff's style has a unique physicality. It is difficult to describe, except to say that the actors use their whole body to communicate. Very little use is made of staging or props, everything being created by the body through mime.

Love or loathe either of these artists, they have created their own captivating STYLE. Similarly, our challenge is to hold an audience in our own preferred way.

Substance

But let us remember the warning to avoid a piece which is all style and no substance. In dramatic art there are limitless ideas for the substance or theme of a piece. This is particularly true of Christian-based work. Sometimes the message a play is trying to communicate is obvious, other times it is not so apparent. In C. P. Taylor's astoundingly brilliant play entitled *Good* we receive a clear and haunting message from a man unwittingly and terrifyingly easily drawn into the Nazi hierarchy. I recently saw a production of this play at the Donmar Warehouse in London and the substance of the piece was communicated with such style that it sent a shiver down my spine. On the other hand, one of my favourite plays of recent years, Conor McPherson's *The Weir,* is seemingly a simple tale of a group of men and one woman talking and sharing ghostly tales in a deserted Irish pub. You could mistakenly accuse this play of seeming rather shallow, but its tremendous impact proves that it does not lack substance.

So what point am I trying to make here? Simply this: while a play or sketch needs to have style and substance to make it interesting to watch, this does not mean that the message immediately has to clout the audience over the head like a lead brick! If at the end of a sketch an obvious point has not been made, with all the loose ends neatly tied up, this does not make it an ineffective piece.

I think, as Christians, we particularly need to absorb this message. Some groups may never consider performing a sketch unless it makes a clear point about the futility of life without God and gives three easy steps on how to have a personal relationship with Jesus. I'm not suggesting that overtly evangelistic sketches are wrong – my last book is stuffed full of them. But there are other forms or styles of drama which can provoke a different kind of reaction.

As time goes by, cultures and methods of communication change in the church as well as outside, and it is important to keep an eye on these changes. For instance, no longer is evangelism seen as merely a seeker-friendly service every few months followed by an altar call, a cup of tea and a packet of custard creams. Although this is one form of outreach, Christians are more aware nowadays of the need for friendship evangelism and relationship building, before leading people to Christ with one-to-one communications. Faith, in other words, is not a neat little package deal, but a living relationship which involves questions and honest discussion. There is a place, then, for Christian sketches which raise questions encouraging discussion, rather than tying up all the loose ends.

Willow Creek's world-famous seeker-friendly services and their style of drama purposely leave unanswered questions which can be picked up on during the teaching and in future discussion. While most pieces in *50 Sketches About Jesus* used the more traditional evangelical drama method, in this book I have gone more for the type of sketch that raises questions rather than giving answers, linking these with a clear teaching point which can be built upon in teaching or discussion.

I don't want to appear all arty by suggesting that having the limitations of communicating a message compromises the art! Anyone who knows me will tell you that's just not my style, and I do passionately believe that we can use drama effectively in communicating the exciting truth of the gospel. But however strongly I believe in the power of drama, it's not often that after seeing a drama a repentant sinner drops to their knees and asks for forgiveness. A response to the gospel will nearly always come later when considering or discussing the things which have been heard. My advice to you, even my plea, is don't be put off by a sketch because it's not a traditional, nice, neat little package. Throw all your creative abilities into putting together and performing the piece, then rely on the power of the art form to do its work in challenging, provoking thought and encouraging discussion.

I recently saw an interview with the brilliant and rather surreal filmmaker, David Lynch. His films often leave questions unanswered (or maybe I'm just a bit simple!) and this has film critics and buffs debating his intentions. In the interview I saw, the guy posing the questions was pushing Lynch as to what he meant by a particular scene in his film *Blue Velvet*, and what we're meant to believe happens to the lead character after the close of the film. I can't quote Lynch's exact response, but basically he was saying he didn't know! What we make of his films is up to us, and as regards what happens next, well, the film finishes when it finishes – end of story. If you decide what you think happens next, that in effect is your own business! I for one was fascinated by his response. What, you may ask, is the point of that? If we don't know what it's all supposed to be about and what happens at the end, it's a waste of time watching it in the first place. For Christian drama this could be argued as a valid point; on the other hand maybe this is the reason Lynch's films are so often discussed and dissected. Surely from an evangelistic perspective, this can only be a good thing.

Improvisation: give it a go!

There you go! I've done it again. In *50 Sketches About Jesus*, I used that scary drama swear word, and here I am again up to my old tricks: IMPROVISATION!

This is not going to be some lengthy exposition on the art of improvisation – territory well covered by others far greater than me. Instead I want to encourage the waverers who need to be converted into believing that they really should GIVE IT A GO!

The root cause of people's reluctance to improvise is that they are petrified of making themselves look a complete prat! We're all friends here together, so let's be totally honest. The fear of having no ideas on a given topic, or even getting going for 30 seconds, and then completely drying up, means that improvisation is often a discipline people tend to avoid. My advice to you is, DON'T! All be very brave; get in a circle; join hands and take deep breaths. (Don't panic, I'm not going all new agey on you!) Make a solemn vow not to laugh at each other and then I want you all to give yourselves

PERMISSION TO LOOK PRUNES!

Now before you all close the book, give up on the idea and accuse me of being the most discouraging human being to walk the earth since my sadistic music teacher, let me expand. I want to squash the vicious rumour that everything created in an improvised setting should be on a par with *Whose line is it anyway?* or always be slick and usable. Yes, some fantastic ideas come out of improvisation exercises, but to be totally frank it's not a very high percentage. Both studying drama and working professionally have afforded me many opportunities to take part in improvisation exercises, but even in these settings the vast majority of words that come forth from your mouth are utter tripe!

The point, then, is not the volume of usable ideas that come from the session, though this can be a very nice sideline, but rather the exercise itself which serves to stretch your creative muscles. It is particularly important to have improvisation exercises when part of a drama group, as they help you learn how the other group members work, which can be useful if you sometimes have to think on your feet. As we all know, however much rehearsal goes into a piece, on occasion things don't go entirely to plan! During these times it is important that the performers are flexible, and can trust one another to pull the piece back together. Having worked together in an improvisation workshop setting will be invaluable at times like this.

I was recently acting in a lavish, high-tech production in York called *Timewarp 2000*. The show had been over a year in planning and the huge stage at the Barbican Hall was graced with a phenomenal set of an alien spaceship. The show was highly technical with an array of sound FX, lighting and pyrotechnics. I won't go into details of the show except to make the point regarding things not always going to plan! During the first performance of the show one of the pyrotechnic explosions set fire to some paper on the stage and in front of over 1,200 children we had the problem of coping with this complete nightmare. It was fantastic to be working with a cast and crew of consummate professionals (I won't mention any names as they'll probably ask for money!) who entered into a couple of minutes of nerve-jangling improvisation to put the fire out and continue with the show. After a short amount of stamping on the fire, throwing things on it and an automatic fire extinguisher coming into operation from the back of the set, we got things back on track with the audience none the wiser. It has to be said, it wasn't one of my most enjoyable moments as an actor, though certainly one of the most memorable!

Now unless you're planning any kind of high-tech production it is unlikely an on-stage fire is something you'll have to deal with. Commonly speaking, a problem with props or remembering lines is where things will most likely go kaput! Improvisation sessions, as well as being a lot of fun and stretching your creative abilities, will help you to work together more effectively in getting yourselves out of an unexpected situation.

Improvising the Proverbs

As I explained in my introduction, there is much in the Proverbs that speaks to different people in different ways, thus making this book of the Bible an ideal resource for improvising. To help you, I have created three lists; they are by no means exhaustive, and with a bit of thought you can add your own suggestions to the ones that I have made.

The first list is the character you must play, the second is the setting in which the action takes place, and the third is a selection of proverbs and themes the improvisation must attempt to communicate. Randomly choose one suggestion from each list, and then split into pairs to get to work. (You can use larger groups depending on numbers in your group and personal preference.) Improvisation is traditionally done totally on the spot, i.e. the volunteers will be given the character, setting and proverb and from this they just make up things as they go along in front of the rest of the group. This is an acceptable way of doing the exercise, but maybe I can encourage you to break the rules slightly, also removing the nagging fear of drowning. Each pair or group is given their selection, and then have a short amount of time (no more than five or ten minutes) to try a few things out together before playing it to the group. This time gap enables the volunteers to discuss and try a few ideas, but without giving them enough time to have any assemblance of a script. Tight time schedules are a good discipline and often produce some really great ideas.

There are limitless possibilities to an exercise like this: exchanging partners, using different-sized groups, prep time of only two minutes, etc. You may find some gems of ideas come out of a session like this, and these can obviously be worked on further maybe to convert into a script. I cannot promise this result, though it has happened on many previous occasions. What I can promise you is a worthwhile and enjoyable evening, and a real sense of achievement at what you can collectively put together. So, are you ready?

List one: characters

The person in charge of the session may decide to begin by giving individuals a character they will be more comfortable with. This is fine, though a random selection can be much more fun. You can make both actors in an exercise the same character, for instance two drunkards or two politicians; alternatively you can mix and match the characters.

1. An old woman.
2. Football hooligan.
3. Seven-year-old.
4. Teenage lad.
5. Drunkard.
6. Fisherman/woman.
7. Market stallholder.
8. Superhero.
9. Cartoon character.
10. Six-month-old baby.
11. Pirate.
12. Country gent.
13. Homeless person.
14. Politician.
15. Vicar.
16. Paparazzi photographer.
17. Upper-class twit.
18. Tarty secretary.
19. Darts player.
20. An elephant!
21. Elvis Presley.
22. Astronaut.
23. 103-year-old.
24. Shoplifter.
25. Noah.

List two: settings

Again, you may decide to begin by pairing an obvious character with a familiar setting, e.g. an old lady in a bingo hall. However, things take on a very interesting and highly amusing turn if you go for random selections.

1. Bingo hall.
2. Theatre foyer.
3. Bus stop.
4. Doctor's surgery.
5. Church.
6. Football stadium.
7. Train carriage.
8. Rollercoaster.
9. Hospital casualty.
10. Library.
11. At the seaside.
12. Nightclub.
13. Ice rink.
14. At the opera.
15. Posh restaurant.
16. Greasy Spoon café.
17. Aeroplane.
18. Supermarket checkout.
19. Back row at the cinema.
20. School playground.
21. In a factory.
22. Stuck in a lift.
23. Hairdressing salon.
24. Chiropodist's.
25. The zoo.

List three: proverbs and themes

With each of the proverbs I have listed, I have given a general theme to give the groups a basic idea of what to communicate. If on reading the proverb the group members see an alternative meaning they would prefer to use, this is okay.

1. Wisdom. Proverbs 19:20.
2. Loyalty. Proverbs 3:3.
3. Envy. Proverbs 14:30.
4. Lying. Proverbs 12:22.
5. Bad Temper. Proverbs 16:32.
6. Friendship. Proverbs 18:24.
7. Boasting. Proverbs 25:6–7.
8. Foolishness. Proverbs 27:22.
9. Oppression. Proverbs 26:22.
10. Prudence. Proverbs 13:16.
11. Temperance. Proverbs 20:1.
12. Dishonest gain. Proverbs 10:2.
13. Wealth. Proverbs 18:11.
14. Bribery. Proverbs 17:23.
15. Helping the poor. Proverbs 19:7.
16. Saving for the future. Proverbs 21:20.
17. Generosity. Proverbs 14:21.
18. Accepting criticism. Proverbs 10:8.
19. Choosing wise friends. Proverbs 14:7.
20. Humility. Proverbs 11:2.
21. Pride. Proverbs 16:18.
22. Laziness. Proverbs 10:4.
23. Uses of the tongue. Proverbs 4:24.
24. Listening to both sides of a story. Proverbs 18:17.
25. Gossiping. Proverbs 26:22.

As I said earlier, you can easily add dozens more ideas to these lists. (The more unlikely, the better!) These are just a selection that I have thought up and used in the past. Some people will respond better to improvisation than others, but it is well worth persevering, as quite often the best ideas come from the most unlikely person.

I hope you enjoy having a go at these exercises to stimulate the creative flow, and also using the 25 ready-to-use sketches, which now follow. Drama has a brilliant and unique way of stimulating people's minds – it's been proved time and time again. I wish you all the best as we join together in trying to communicate ancient and challenging truths in new and exciting ways.

Armchair Manager

Where there is no vision, the people will perish.

INTRODUCTION

This instantly recognisable proverb, in my humble opinion, packs its best punch in the Authorised Version of the Bible. To illustrate the point, I have used a hopeless football manager, sending out his team with no plan or vision. (This is no reflection on my personal opinion of the current England manager.) The sketch starts with two couples debating during a televised match, and moves into a scene with a boss and his players during team tactics. The two couples become the four players and much can be made of this transition. The first half of the sketch acts as an aperitif leading into the second half where the point about the importance of having a vision is made. The sketch can stand alone or will work well with teaching on leadership and vision. Given the fast-changing nature of the England line-up, you can easily update the piece with minor rewrites introducing current players.

Characters: BARRY, KEITH, TAMMY, WENDY, BOSS.

Lights come up. BARRY and KEITH are sitting stage left watching football on TV. TAMMY and WENDY are sitting stage right, half-watching and chatting. BOSS is standing behind them in front of a blackboard. He remains frozen until the second half of the sketch. As the lights come up BARRY and KEITH are getting excited as a goal is about to be scored. Unfortunately the striker misses.

x

27

BARRY: Oh, I don't believe it!

KEITH: How could he miss that – it was a sitter.

BARRY: 'Cos he's a donkey Keith, a grade A donkey!

TAMMY: Not bad looking though eh Wend...? (*They laugh*)

BARRY: Ah, shut it you two.

TAMMY: Ooh, temper temper!

BARRY: You two drive me nuts, chatting all the way through it. This is an important game.

TAMMY: Well I'm sorry for breathing. Bloomin' cheek!

WENDY: Yeah, what do you expect us to do – sit here in silence?

KEITH: No, he never asked for a miracle.

WENDY: Don't get larey Keith, or I'll give you some of that. (*She holds up a fist*)

KEITH: Woo, I'm scared.

BARRY: (*Stands shouting*) OH WHAT!! Did you see that?

KEITH: No, I missed it; what happened?

BARRY: (*Yells at TV*) You're supposed to kick it, not trip over it, you big div bag!

KEITH: I reckon we could do better than this bunch.

TAMMY: Oh yeah, right!

BARRY: My dad could play better than this lot, my grandad even, and he's been dead since 1972.

KEITH: Our problem's that manager; he hasn't got a clue about team selection. Now if I were in charge. . . .

WENDY: Oh here we go, the armchair managers.

KEITH: Keep your nose out, frizz ball, this is men's talk.

WENDY: Oh we'll keep out of it then and discuss cross-stitch patterns.

KEITH: Yeah, you do that. As I was saying Barry, his selection's all wrong. For a start he wants to get shot of Shearer.

BARRY: Get shot of Shearer! You're having a laugh Keith.

KEITH: No, he's well past his sell-by date Baz. Give him credit, in his prime he was good, but he's lost it.

BARRY: No, no, no, no, no. Anyhow, who are you gonna put in?

KEITH: Well you got Cole, Owen and loads of young blood coming through. It ain't a big problem.

BARRY: Granted, Keith. But it's not Shearer's fault. The problem is he ain't getting the service.

TAMMY: Ooh, I wouldn't mind giving Shearer some service!

WENDY: Eugh Tams, he's well old.

TAMMY: He's not old, just mature.

WENDY: Whatever he is, he's completely rank.

TAMMY: Ooh, I love it when he takes his shirt off to swap at the end of a game. I go all tingly.

BARRY: Have you two finished drooling? We was having a serious discussion here.

TAMMY: Well, don't let us stop you.

BARRY: Thank you. As I was saying, Keith, we're all right in defence and up front, but in the midfield area we're just not pushing through and giving the service to our front boys.

KEITH: Ah come on Baz, what about the boy Beckham? He chucks them in with pinpoint accuracy.

BARRY: Yeah, Beckham's all right I suppose, when he can stop fiddling with his hair, but it can't all fall to him, can it?

WENDY: Ooh, I'd fall to him anyway.

BARRY: Oh blimey, they're off again!

WENDY: Well, you must admit he is absolutely lush.

TAMMY: Huh, he only looks about twelve.

WENDY: Oh I don't care, I love them boyish looks.

BARRY: Pity you ended up with Keith then, ha ha!

KEITH: Get lost.

TAMMY: No, I prefer a proper man.

BARRY: (*To KEITH*) Not a word.

TAMMY: That Beckham only needs to shave once a fortnight.

WENDY: Well I don't care what you think, I reckon Victoria
Spice is a lucky woman.

BARRY: You have a point, Wendy. Whatever anyone says
about David Beckham, give the boy credit, at the
end of the day he goes home to Posh Spice. Look
at me, I get indoors to find Scary Spice over there
with her curlers in!

TAMMY: Get lost, you ugly spud!

BARRY: Oh come on, you love me really.

TAMMY: In your dreams I do. You're just a fill in till I find
someone decent.

BARRY: Ooh, bitchy bitchy!

WENDY: What colour shirts did you say we was?

KEITH: I hate it when women ask that. How many times
have I got to tell you? WHITE!

WENDY: Oh. Well, I just thought I'd tell you the reds have
just scored.

BARRY/KEITH: WHAT!!

TAMMY: Oh what a shame, boys.

BARRY: Oh no, we're stuffed.

KEITH: That's the finals next summer out the window.

BARRY: It's that manager's fault.

KEITH: He's got no vision.

BARRY: He's even worse than the last one, if that's possible.

KEITH: And where there is no vision, the players will perish.

TAMMY\WENDY\BARRY: (*Together*) What?!

KEITH: If they don't know where they're supposed to be

going, how are they ever going to get there?

TAMMY\WENDY\BARRY: (*Together*) Oh!

BOSS: (*He claps to get team's attention. BARRY, KEITH, TAMMY and WENDY turn around. As they turn back on audience they have got players' names on their backs. They have now become four players.*) Right . . . well, let's get sorted, shall we? All right are we?

ALL: Yes, Boss.

BOSS: Good, so let's go and . . . go and . . . well, you know, go and win!

BARRY: How are we gonna do that, Boss?

BOSS: I beg your pardon?

BARRY: How are we going to win?

KEITH: What's the plan?

TAMMY: The strategy.

WENDY: Tactics.

BOSS: (*Pause*) Ah yes, tactics. Good point, tactics, team tactics . . . erm, any suggestions?

BARRY: Well you're the boss, Boss. We follow your intrepid leadership. Your vision.

BOSS: Yes of course, my vision. Absolutely first class, top notch, good point. . . . Don't suppose any of you could give me a clue at all?

KEITH: Scoring goals is a good place to start, Boss.

BOSS: GOALS! Of course, excellent. . . . (*Starts drawing nonsensical diagrams on blackboard*) Well the other team have a goal, and our players, that's you, have to kick the ball into their goal, to score, so we win.

TAMMY: Brilliant.

WENDY: Absolutely fantastic, Boss.

KEITH: You really are a masterful tactician.

BOSS: Well, you're too kind.

BARRY: But how do we get there, Boss?

BOSS: There's always one, isn't there! Well, it's a fair point I suppose. You've noticed the slight glitch in my plan – well spotted. Well, how about if you get the ball to start with, is that all right?

BARRY: If you say so, Boss.

BOSS: (*Continues drawing*) Good, then if you pass it to say . . . erm . . . (*Looks at Wendy*) how about you?

WENDY: Fine with me, Boss.

BOSS: Excellent. You play with it for a bit, then chuck it over to him.

KEITH: Okey dokey.

BOSS: And then for our *coup de grâce*, and I think you'll like this, you pass it to him.

TAMMY: Yeah.

BOSS: And then you stick it in the goal. Easy as that. So to recap, it's you to you to you to you, and then into the goal. You don't look convinced.

BARRY: The plan seems just a touch on the loose side, Boss.

BOSS: Well of course it's loose; anything can happen out there – you have to be flexible. You can't expect me to do everything for you. Now quickly, let's run through one more time. Who starts?

BARRY: Me.

BOSS: Good, and he passes it to?

WENDY: Me.

BOSS: And then?

KEITH: Me.

BOSS: Wonderful, and then finally?

TAMMY: Me, Boss.

BOSS: And what do you do with it?

TAMMY: Stick it in the goal, Boss.

BOSS: Fantastic! Well, what are you waiting for? The game's about to start; chop chop! (*Players exit mumbling. BOSS looks at diagram, pleased with himself*) I don't know what they're worrying about. It can't fail. (*BOSS exits, fade to blackout*)

TEACHING POINT

The need in the church for strong leaders with a clear vision.

BIBLE REFERENCE

Proverbs 29:18

Communication Breakdown

A wicked messenger falls into trouble, but a trustworthy envoy brings healing.

INTRODUCTION

If there's one thing in the church, workplace and home that causes us endless problems it's poor communication. Whether an individual is giving misguidance on purpose, or whether it is purely an innocent case of communication breakdown, the results can be catastrophic. This sketch serves to illustrate this point, the problem beginning with the simple case of a couple not listening to each other, further compounded by a poor phone line when their son phones from France.

During rehearsal the cast should build up the confusion between the characters as they shout at each other and raise voices down the phone line. If performed well this sketch should prove really frustrating for the audience to watch.

Although Terry will obviously share the same stage, he is meant to be miles away. Position him carefully and serve the point by maybe using a backdrop of France, and props such as a beret or string of onions.

Characters: MOTHER, FATHER, TERRY.

Lights come up on FATHER, sitting and watching TV. MOTHER is offstage.

FATHER: (*Talking to TV*) Cor blimey, mate, I wouldn't risk it if I were you. Take the money and run . . . Ooh, he's gone for C, a flying amphibian. He'll regret that.

34

MOTHER: (*Calling from offstage*) Do you wanna beer, Father?

FATHER: (*Concentrating on TV*) Mmm?

MOTHER: I said do you wanna beer?

FATHER: Grow a beard? What do I wanna grow a beard for?

MOTHER: (*Enters*) Not a beard. A beer. B-E-E-R.

FATHER: Oh yeah, yeah ... ta ... (*MOTHER exits, FATHER talks to TV*) Ooh, he has; he's done it. Not C, you idiot.

MOTHER: (*Re-enters*) Not what?

FATHER: What?

MOTHER: What did you just say?

FATHER: Oh, nothing.

MOTHER: Yes you did.

FATHER: Not to you! The TV, the TV. It's ... oh forget it.

MOTHER: So you still wanna beer?

FATHER: Mmm?

MOTHER: You still wanna beer?

FATHER: Yes! Yes! (*MOTHER exits, FATHER mutters*) Flipping woman.

MOTHER: (*Calling from offstage*) What one?

FATHER: Well of course I want one. I don't want six. I'm not a flipping alcoholic.

MOTHER: Not want one, as in the number, what one as in Stella, Heineken or Guinness.

FATHER: Oh I see. Whatever, just whatever. I'm trying to concentrate. Women! You can't live with 'em, you can't live without 'em ... Oh. look at that; I don't believe it. It was a flying amphibian. (*Calls out*) Hey Mother, he just won 125,000 quid.

MOTHER: (*Rushes in excited*) You've just won 125,000 quid?

FATHER: What?

MOTHER: You've won 125,000 quid?

FATHER: No! Not me, you daft moose. HIM! I could have won 125,000 quid if I was on there. I knew the answer was a flying amphibian all along.

MOTHER: (*Passes him a Guinness*) Oh well, drown your sorrows with that.

FATHER: Guinness! Oh, I fancied a lager.

MOTHER: Oh I give up. (*TERRY enters and starts dialling phone*)

FATHER: Hello, here we go. This one's for quarter of a million. (*Phone rings, both ignore for a few rings*) Your turn, love.

MOTHER: (*Reluctantly answers phone*) Hello.

TERRY: (*Speaks loudly*) Hello, Mum.

MOTHER: (*Shouts*) HELLO!

FATHER: Oi, Ssshhh!!…(*Indicates TV*)

MOTHER: Well, I can't hear! Hello, who is it?

TERRY: Mum, it's me, TERRY.

MOTHER: (*Pause*) No, I'm sorry, love, we're fully double glazed.

TERRY: MUM! TERRY, YOUR SON TERRY!!

MOTHER: Terry! Is that you? Ooh, Father, it's Terry.

FATHER: Great.

MOTHER: It's a terrible line, Terry; I can hardly hear you.

FATHER: Where is he?

MOTHER: Where are you?

TERRY: I'm calling from a call box in Calais.

MOTHER: Rally! . . . (*To Father*) Something about a rally.

FATHER: Well that'll explain the bad line – all them rowdy cars screaming by.

TERRY: Are you still there?

MOTHER: Hello.

TERRY: Listen, Mum, I'm in France with a friend. Can Dad come and get me from Dover ferry port with Nick?

MOTHER: (*Confused*) Did you say can Dad come and ferry you home from the nick?

FATHER: (*Chokes on drink*) WHAT! What's he doing in the nick?

MOTHER: Oh blimey, Terry, what are you doing in the nick?

TERRY: What am I doing with Nick? We're in France.

MOTHER: They're in a trance.

FATHER: A trance! Oh no, he's back on them flipping drugs again. Is that how he got arrested?

MOTHER: Is that how you got arrested?

TERRY: Am I well rested? Er, well not really, but if Dad picks me up, I'll get rested when I'm back home.

MOTHER: Apparently you've got to pick him up and he'll be arrested when he's back home.

FATHER: Oh KIDS!! Who'd have 'em. Give me that phone. (*He shouts down phone*) TERRY! Which nick are you in?

TERRY: Which nick? My old pal from school, NICK HORRIDGE.

FATHER: NORWICH! What the blazes are you doing in Norwich?

TERRY: WHAT?

FATHER: What the blazes are . . . oh forget it. I'll come and get you.

TERRY: I CAN'T HEAR.

FATHER: I'LL COME AND GET YOU.

TERRY: Great! So recap, it's from the ferry at Dover.

FATHER: Yes, I'll ferry you over.

TERRY: With Nick Horridge.

FATHER: Nick at Norwich.

TERRY: Our sailing's set for 09.00 hours.

FATHER: Your bail's been set at nine hundred pounds. Oh, stone the living crows. I'M ON MY WAY! (*Slams down phone*)

TERRY: I'll see you in the morning. (*He shrugs and puts phone down, then exits*)

FATHER: (*Rushing*) Coat, car keys, cheque book. I need to get a shift on. If I don't get to Norwich soon he'll be behind bars ... (*Pauses to look at TV*) Five hundred thousand, the lucky moose! (*Lights fade to blackout*)

TEACHING POINT

The importance of honest and reliable communication, and the consequences of failure.

BIBLE REFERENCE

Proverbs 13:17

The Future, Charles
(But Not as We Know It)

There is surely a future hope for you, and your hope will not be cut off.

INTRODUCTION

This sketch, set around the turn of the new century, looks at our hope for the future and where we place it. Humans put their future hope in a variety of things, as illustrated during the start of the new millennium, with end-of-the-world prophecies and the proposed effect of the infamous Millennium Bug. However, our real hope for the future should lie elsewhere, as stated in Proverbs 23 and 24.

Set at the precise moment we moved from 1999 into 2000, the sketch looks at a couple who are expecting some fantastic bolt of lightning. When nothing happens they are forced to consider new possibilities for the future of themselves and the world.

Characters: CHARLES, JENNIFER.

Lights come up on CHARLES and JENNIFER. There is a TV, video, toaster, etc. around set. We hear the midnight chimes of Big Ben, followed by distant cheering and a chorus of Auld Lang Syne. CHARLES is frantically looking at the electrical appliances, and out of the window JENNIFER is looking on in disgusted boredom.

CHARLES: Nothing!
JENNIFER: Oh surprise, surprise!
CHARLES: Not a flipping sausage.

39

JENNIFER: Well, what did you really expect, Charles?

CHARLES: Eh?

JENNIFER: What did you expect? Big Ben to welcome in the new millennium and then spontaneously explode, along with our microwave oven and Breville sandwich toaster?

CHARLES: I don't know what I expected exactly, but I thought something would happen.

JENNIFER: It did. Millions of people celebrated the dawn of a new era with champagne and party poppers. But not us. We sat in here watching Angus Deayton and pondering the onslaught of Armageddon.

CHARLES: Well, you can't be too careful, can you Jennifer? There's been dozens of predictions recently saying that at the stroke of midnight, the middle of the earth will boil and the skies will fall in. I mean, you wouldn't want to be out on a night like that, would you?

JENNIFER: Oh, come off it Charles; you're so gullible. They're just a bunch of fraudsters – they'll be back on telly tomorrow reading the stars. I had my palm read by one of them years back. She said, 'You'll marry a handsome millionaire and live in a secluded mansion.' Silly moo made a right pig's ear out of that, didn't she? I got a balding tobacconist and a damp-infested bungalow.

CHARLES: Ah, but these aren't some cranky end-of-pier fortune-tellers! They're proper TV experts.

JENNIFER: Oh heaven deliver us from TV experts! One minute they're on a soap opera or some naff quiz show, and the next thing you know they're being set up as the font of all knowledge on healthy lifestyle, whatever that might be!

CHARLES: Ooh, Carol Vorderman knows all about that.

JENNIFER: Don't get me started on Carol 'know-it-all' Vorderman.

CHARLES: Anyway, forget all the end-of-the-world stuff; what about that Millennium Bug? What was all that fuss about?

JENNIFER: A clever marketing ploy to get you to buy a new computer.

CHARLES: Don't be such a cynic, Jennifer. We had brochures through the post, Sunday newspaper supplements, the works. I thought the stock markets would freefall and credit companies go into overload losing all record of wealth. An instant state of anarchy.

JENNIFER: Ooh, you really are thick sometimes.

CHARLES: Thank you, darling.

JENNIFER: You've been watching too many of those futuristic films, haven't you! They've been planning the millennium effect for years. However inept our governments can be, I'm sure they wouldn't allow a shift in the calendar to spark off a socialist revolution.

CHARLES: Well if they're so organised, how come they reckon loads of videos will go berserk?

JENNIFER: What are you on about now?

CHARLES: They can send men to the moon, they can build a telescope to look at the stars in minute detail, but they can't manage a video that understands the concept of the year 2000.

JENNIFER: You're mad.

CHARLES: Mad, am I? We'll see, my little darling. Would

you mind checking that our state of the art VCR is recording, as requested, the *Jools Holland New Year Hootenanny*?

JENNIFER: (*Checks video*) Oh blimey, you're right. It isn't.

CHARLES: The Millennium Bug strikes. QED. I rest my case.

JENNIFER: You programmed it to tape Channel 4, you big div!

CHARLES: What?

JENNIFER: It's recording, as requested ... (*Checks TV times*) ... some arty foreign film.

CHARLES: Oh, I've never got the hang of that stupid timer.

JENNIFER: I told you to spend the extra twenty quid and get the 'video plus' thingy. But no, you knew best.

CHARLES: (*Pause*) Well, that's that then.

JENNIFER: Yep.

CHARLES: The year 2000 and everything's exactly the same.

JENNIFER: 'Fraid so.

CHARLES: No buildings have collapsed to our knowledge, the sky's still in its right place up there, and I still can't work that poxy video.

JENNIFER: Well, that's a comforting thought.

CHARLES: No one really knows what's coming next, do they? So, how do we know what to expect, what to hope for?

JENNIFER: The future, Charles.

CHARLES: Mmm, so what's that got in store for us then?

JENNIFER: I don't know. Maybe the future's not been written yet and we just make it up as we go along. Or maybe it has been written but it's not the stargazers and TV experts that have all the answers. Those answers might be found elsewhere.

CHARLES: You could be right. In the meantime, Happy New Millennium, darling.

JENNIFER: And to you. (*They pick up glasses and clink them together*) Here's to our future, Charles.

CHARLES: But not as we know it. . . . (*Futuristic film soundtrack builds up and CHARLES and JENNIFER gaze up confused. Blackout*)

TEACHING POINT

Where do you place your hope and assurance for the future?

BIBLE REFERENCES

Proverbs 23:18; 24:14

Gloria

Laziness brings on deep sleep, and the shiftless man goes hungry.

INTRODUCTION

One of my favourite characters in theatre is Captain Boyle in Sean O'Casey's *Juno and the Paycock*. In this sketch Jim's laziness and refusal to get a job are reminiscent of Captain Boyle, although the circumstance is very different. Lazy characters are traditionally quite funny and loveable, but in this there can be the danger of playing down the stark effects laziness can have on life and relationships. In Proverbs 19:15 we are challenged to look at the effects of laziness and warned against it. The sketch starts as a funny account of family life, but should build to a much more serious conclusion. This is what the actors and director should aim for.

Characters: JIM, GLORIA, PAUL, KYLIE.

Lights come up on JIM who is sleeping on a chair, centre stage, with a newspaper over his face. PAUL and KYLIE enter; PAUL is in the middle of telling a joke.

PAUL: So this woman says to him, 'What's up with you?' right. And he says, and here's the punchline, 'I'm an extractor fan.' (*Pause, KYLIE has obviously not got the joke*) Don't you get it?

KYLIE: I don't think so, no.

PAUL: He was an ex-tractor fan. It's obvious innit? EX … TRACTOR … FAN! See . . . oh forget it; you're hopeless you are.

KYLIE: Oh yeah, I think I get it now. An extractor fan. Ha
            ha. Yeah, good one, Paul. I like it.

PAUL: You're useless, you are. You never get jokes, even
            when they're dead easy ones.

KYLIE: I do, sometimes. . . . (*PAUL gives her a knowing
            look*) Oh shut up and make us a cup of tea.

PAUL: Yeah, all right. . . . (*He notices JIM*) Cor blimey;
            look, there's a vision if ever I saw one.

KYLIE: What?

PAUL: Dad, sitting on his *derrière* doing sweet Fanny
            Adams.

KYLIE: Yeah, he's always sat there when I come round.

PAUL: He's always sat there, period! His posterior is per-
            manently superglued to that chair, and try as you
            might, you can't shift him.

KYLIE: Really?

PAUL: Honestly. If you don't believe me, have a go.

KYLIE: What?

PAUL: Have a go at getting him to shift.

KYLIE: How?

PAUL: Down to you. You can use any method except for
            physical contact.

KYLIE: Oh I don't know, I feel silly.

PAUL: All right, I'll go first to get you started. Right, lis-
            ten to this. . . . (*He maniacally screams and runs
            around room*) FIRE! FIRE! FIRE! Quick Dad, the
            house is burning down, we're all gonna die! CALL
            999! CALL 999!! (*He stops, they stare at JIM who
            has not so much as moved*) See, nothing. Your
            turn.

KYLIE: Oh, I can't think . . . erm . . . Mr Miller, Mr Miller,
            there's someone at the door for you.

PAUL: No, no, no! There's someone at the door for you! Come on Kylie, you can do better than that. Remember this lump is as dormant as Mount Etna!

KYLIE: Okay, erm. . . . QUICK, MR MILLER, IT'S WORLD WAR III, WORLD WAR III; THE RUSSIANS HAVE INVADED; ONLY FIVE MINUTES TO LIVE; QUICK!! (*Still no movement*)

PAUL: Better, much better, but Dad doesn't consider anything that happens outside these four walls as being any of his business. No, you need to know what buttons to push. There's only one thing on this planet that gets Dad to move.

KYLIE: What's that then?

PAUL: Guess.

KYLIE: I haven't got a clue.

PAUL: Guess.

KYLIE: The DSS calling round.

PAUL: No.

KYLIE: Carol Vorderman on the telly.

PAUL: No.

KYLIE: A win on the lottery.

PAUL: No, he's too lazy to walk down the shop to enter it.

KYLIE: I give up, Paul; go on tell me.

PAUL: All right. Are you ready for this? . . . (*Pause for big effect*) Dad, Mum's coming.

JIM: (*Immediately sits up in a panic*) What! When! Where!

PAUL: See, I told you. It works every time.

JIM: Paul, stop talking cryptic. Where's your mother?

PAUL: Calm down, she's not here. I was just proving a point to Kylie.

JIM: Proving a point! You little toe rag; you nearly give me a heart attack.

KYLIE: Afternoon, Mr Miller.

JIM: Hello Kylie, love. I don't know what a lovely girl like you is doing hanging around the likes of him.

PAUL: (*Mock offence*) Him! I'm your only son and heir, Pater.

JIM: Don't give me all that Pater nonsense. I'm still in a state of palpitation here with the fear that Gloria was arriving. What are you two up to anyway?

PAUL: Oh, we were just gonna make a drink, then go upstairs to do our homework.

JIM: Do our homework! Is that what they call it nowadays, eh?

PAUL: Dad, give it a rest will you?

GLORIA: (*Offstage*) Hello! Anybody home? (*All give look of animated shock*)

JIM: Gloria! (*He madly tries to tidy up around his chair, hiding beer cans, dirty plates and cups etc.*) Quick, I'm dead meat.

GLORIA: (*Enters*) Goodness me, a house full. Hello Paul, Kylie.

KYLIE: Hello Mrs Miller.

GLORIA: Oh hello Jim. I didn't expect to find you here.

JIM: You only just about did, my love. What I mean to say is, that as it happens I erm . . . I've only just got in myself.

GLORIA: Oh is that right?

JIM: Paul and Kylie will back me up on that, won't you?

PAUL: (*Pause*) We're just going up to do our homework, aren't we, Kylie?

KYLIE: Yeah, that's right, we are. Bye Mr Miller, Mrs Miller. Nice to see you again.

GLORIA: You too, Kylie. Enjoy your homework, and no loud

music.

JIM: Kids! Busy day, love?

GLORIA: Busier than some, I've no doubt. . . . (*She sits down*)

JIM: Ah come on, love, how about a nice cup of tea? (*JIM gets up and a pain strikes his knee*) Oh, my knee. My cursed knee. I'm an absolute martyr to it . . . . (*Pauses for sympathy, GLORIA reads magazine*) Well, are you not going to say anything, words of sympathy or the like?

GLORIA: No.

JIM: Well, would you credit it? Even my own wife doesn't care about my afflictions.

GLORIA: Jim, it's not an affliction, it's just seized up from lack of activity, that's all. . . . I'll put the kettle on. (*GLORIA goes to kitchen*) How did the job hunting go today, need I ask?

JIM: (*He picks up paper and pen and makes some hurried markings*) Oh, not so bad. I've been hours poring over the paper; nearly cross-eyed I am.

GLORIA: (*Enters*) Anything any good?

JIM: Ooh, I've underlined a few possibles.

GLORIA: Let's have a look then.

JIM: Well, later. Let's have a cuppa and discuss it over that.

GLORIA: (*Sternly*) GIVE! (*JIM reluctantly hands over paper*) Ah, what's this one then? Part-time manicurist and pedicurist required for thriving beauty parlour. Experience and references essential. Please contact Miss Mary Benson etc. etc. Well, I think you've got a strong chance of getting that one, Jim. I'm sure your chewed nails and bent over toes will bowl Miss Benson over at the interview.

(GLORIA goes back to kitchen. JIM examines his nails and feet in silence. GLORIA returns with drinks)

JIM: Gloria, love, I am trying my best, honest.

GLORIA: No Jim, you're not. You must think I'm a fool. I know you've been sat here all day, eating, drinking and sleeping. It's pathetic. Do you think I was born yesterday?

JIM: I can't help the plague of unemployment that engulfs the country, love.

GLORIA: Jim, I know there are hundreds of thousands of people in this country genuinely unemployed. It's just that you're not one of them.

JIM: Yes, but I….

GLORIA: *(Interrupts)* No buts. I can't cope with this much longer, Jim. It's all a big joke, isn't it? Jovial Jim lazing around all day, has a few pints and a big laugh at the old dragon Gloria who's trying to drain him of life and drag him into the real world. It's got to stop.

JIM: Sorry.

GLORIA: Sorry's not good enough. Sorry doesn't put grub in the cupboards. I can barely afford enough food to feed one person, let alone three, especially when one of them's you. You know you're a skilled worker, Jim. You know you could go out now, or even pick up the phone and get a job as easy as that. I need you to do it, Jim, and do it fast.

JIM: I know, I know. . . . I'll go tomorrow, I promise.

GLORIA: Really?

JIM: Yeah, I promise. . . . *(Lights fade to blackout)*

TEACHING POINT

Lazy people cause many pains.

BIBLE REFERENCE

Proverbs 19:15

The Greatest Mistake in History

A wicked man accepts a bribe in secret to pervert the course of justice.

INTRODUCTION

To illustrate a proverb about bribery, who better to turn to than Judas Iscariot? Often a figure of debate, people are unsure whether to hate him or feel sorry for him. One thing about Judas we cannot ignore, though, is that he was a thief who accepted a bribe and betrayed Jesus into the hands of his enemies. This piece is set in the period just before Judas attempts to return his money to the authorities. We can only speculate about the state of his mind at this time, but this monologue attempts to expose the dangers of greed and bribery and the reality of our commitment to Christ – leaving the audience to make up their own minds about Judas. A strong actor is required to perform this sketch.

A musical introduction, then lights focus on JUDAS who is holding a money bag, centre stage. As the music stops he drops the bag and addresses the audience directly.

JUDAS: Evil? Me? Well, maybe – I suppose it depends on your perspective. It's an understandable opinion, but are you sure you've been furnished with all the facts, the truth, the whole truth and nothing but the truth as they say? Maybe, maybe not; so you should listen.

For starters, think on this. I was, and I suppose to a certain extent I still am, one of the chosen Twelve. The Master

51

could have chosen from literally thousands of possibles, but
no, he chose me. Judas. Why? Hmm, why? If he knew what
I was going to do, why did he choose me? For fun, for the
challenge – or to fulfil his purpose? Or maybe he did not
know that I would betray him. Maybe he made a mistake.
Oh, but then there is a problem: the Master never makes
mistakes. Faith in him is founded on his having no imper-
fections. So, there is our first dilemma. Why not choose
another one like the other eleven saints – although they
were far from perfect, let me tell you? I admit, maybe I
betrayed him, but all the others abandoned him in his hour
of most need. Ah! When the going gets tough, huh? If you
can't stand the heat. No! But that is them; I must accept my
position. I admit I did accept a bribe; I did betray my
Master.

People curse me, and ask me: Judas, what reason did you
have to betray him? Reason? Well, that's easy. It wasn't
personal – I loved him. He had always been so kind to me,
shown me respect, given me responsibility, accepted me . . .
no, the reason is a lot more basic . . . money. The root of all
. . . ah, you know. The trouble with the Master is his perfec-
tion makes him so misunderstood. All of us have been
guilty of misunderstanding him. I joined with him to lead a
political rebellion, anarchy! Overturn our hopeless and cor-
rupt government, create a new political order; net result –
untold riches. Unfortunately the rebellion he spoke of was
of a peaceful nature, the treasure of a heavenly kind. These
things were not in my vocabulary. Not what I signed up for
. . . Ah, but Judas, the people say. You are a common thief,
you had your hand in the purse of your friends for years.
Yes, I took money. I accepted the bribery of my conscience
but was I not justified? How many of you would work for

nothing? How many of you would go to your office or factory or field and at the end of the week expect to receive no money! Ah, none of you. Yes, I took money, but I worked my fingers to the bone for it. I took what I rightfully earned . . . and it was still a pittance.

When man allows greed to take hold of him, he is open, he is vulnerable to an act of bribery. How were the plans hatched? For me – one so close to the Master – it was simple, so simple. A dimly lit garden, an appointed hour, a Judas kiss . . . ah, it's history. Not only was I being bribed, no, I think I too was trying to bribe. Trying to bribe the Master into using his power, force his hand so to speak into an act of rebellion. As the authorities come, I thought, maybe he will strike back, rebel against them, set into action the course of events I so longed for. Peter, impulsive as ever, struck first. Swish, he sliced an ear off one of the party; there was screaming and blood everywhere. The Master calmly as ever reached over to touch the man; he was instantly healed. Put your sword away, he said; all who draw the sword will die by the sword . . . I knew then my dream was over. As he was led away we exchanged a glance, the final time he looked upon me, and I admit I felt a pang of guilt. I should feel happy. Look what I was left with: the bag of money, fully earned, untold riches. But now I have it, well . . . I can't help feeling that I have just made a terrible mistake. Maybe the greatest mistake in history.

So what do you make of Judas? Is he the villain? Do you hate him for betraying the Master, one so innocent and deserving of loyalty? Is he the fool and you pity him for drawing this dreadful lot in life, unaware of what he was doing, a pawn in a plan over which he had no control? Or maybe for you he is the hero – the man who unwittingly or otherwise assisted in finishing the Master's earthly mission, helping fulfil his destiny? I do not know.

I do know that this money, this bribe now I have it, gives me no pleasure. I have resolved to return it to the authorities now, explain my mistake, clear my name – but I fear it is too late. As I look at my time with the Master, I am not worried that our relationship has been lost; I worry that we never had one in the first place. Some people call me the Son of Hell. If that is true I must be truly evil. The Son of Hell – maybe the price attached to this bribery is the loss of my own soul. . . . The authorities must know how I feel. I will leave immediately. (*He takes bag of money and exits. Music to end as lights fade to blackout*)

TEACHING POINT

Could anything or anyone bribe you to turn your back on Christ?

BIBLE REFERENCE

Proverbs 17:23

Hiding the Forbidden Fruit

He who conceals his sins does not prosper.

INTRODUCTION

This, the first of two sketches based on Proverbs 28:13, looks at the first half of the couplet about hiding our sins from God. The next sketch emphasises accepting responsibility for what we do.

The whole idea of hiding things from God – when we think about it – seems absolutely ridiculous, yet it is something we all attempt to do at some time in our lives. The image of Adam and Eve hiding apple cores behind their backs is no less ridiculous than our own efforts to conceal our sins from God.

In this piece, God is a voice-over, preferably miked up from offstage. There is great comic value in spending time creating costumes for Adam and Eve from bin liners, leaves and other items. Although obviously humorous, God's final speech expelling Adam and Eve should carry some weight reflecting its import. The style of comedy should be frenetic, often farce-like, as Adam and Eve attempt to cover up their obvious disobedience.

Characters: ADAM, EVE, GOD (voice only).

Lights come up on ADAM who is singing while making a covering for himself with leaves. He is wearing a bin liner. An apple core is on the floor.

ADAM: (*Singing*) I'm gonna wash that girl right out of my hair, and send her on her way. . . .

GOD: (*Offstage voice*) Adam.

ADAM: AAGGGHHH!! (*Jumps up and tries to cover himself*) Oh, hello God.

GOD: Are you all right, Adam?

ADAM: (*Nervously*) Yes God, fine God, everything's absolutely ticketyboo, God.

GOD: (*Doubtful*) Adam!

ADAM: What?

GOD: What have you been up to?

ADAM: Nothing!

GOD: Are you sure?

ADAM: Dib dib dib, dob dob dob; Scout's promise.

GOD: Why are you covering yourself up then?

ADAM: Eh . . . erm, ah good question. . . . Well, what with you being the Lord of all creation, I thought it was a bit disrespectful walking around in the buff, so I thought I'd, you know, kit myself out a bit. . . .

GOD: It never bothered you before. I was perfectly happy – it was how I created you.

ADAM: Fair point, God, but between you and me . . . well, it's a bit cold and I got a bit embarrassed, if you know what I mean.

GOD: Embarrassed?

ADAM: Yeah, just a bit. What with Eve being around.

GOD: How can you be embarrassed, Adam? I haven't taught you the concept of embarrassment.

ADAM: Ah, you've got me there.

GOD: Have you been eating the fruit from the tree of knowledge?

ADAM: Me, God? No, God, of course not, God.

GOD: Where did that apple core come from then?

ADAM: (*Shock as he sees apple core; he steps on it*) What apple core is that then, God?

GOD: The one under your foot.

ADAM: (*Lifts other foot*) Nothing there, God.

GOD: The other one.

ADAM: (*Reluctantly lifts foot, feigns shock at sight of apple*) Oh! Ah, that one?

GOD: Yes, Adam, that one.

ADAM: Ah ... yes ... well, erm ... ha ha ... you see that belongs to Eve.

GOD: Pardon?

ADAM: (*Raises voice*) It was Eve's!

EVE: (*Offstage*) Did you call me?

ADAM: (*He jumps*) Aagghh! Yes ... no ... I. ...

EVE: Oh, make your mind up. Look, are you decent yet? If I have to see you walking around starkers any more, I'll end up throwing my apple up all over the place.

ADAM: Ssshhh!

EVE: Don't sshh me!

ADAM: Well, keep your trap shut then; we've got a guest.

EVE: Who? If it's that serpent you can tell him to hiss off.

ADAM: No, it's not the serpent.

EVE: Well, who is it then? This is supposed to be a garden of tranquillity!

ADAM: Just come and see for yourself.

EVE: Are you sure you're decent?

ADAM: YES!!

EVE: All right, I'm coming ... (*EVE enters, smoking and eating an apple*) Come on then, who is it? WELL?

GOD: Hello, Eve.

EVE: (*Spits out apple, chokes, stamps on cigarette and hides apple behind her back*) Ooh, hello God, what a lovely surprise.

GOD: Nice outfit, Eve.

EVE: Oh thank you, God; I've just knocked it up as part of my new summer range.

GOD: Eve.

EVE: Mmm?

GOD: What's that behind your back?

EVE: That! It's just a big cowardy cowardy custard, God; you get used to him after a while.

GOD: No, not Adam. I mean what's in your hand?

EVE: (*Holds out one hand*) Nothing.

GOD: Here we go again. The other one.

EVE: (*Switches apple and holds out other hand*) Nothing there either.

GOD: Both together.

EVE: (*Reluctantly brings out both hands*) Ooh, where did that come from!

GOD: I would hazard a guess at the tree of knowledge.

EVE: Ah, you know ... Well, God, it wasn't strictly my fault; it was that stupid serpent, slithering around promising us all sorts. He's a right pain.

GOD: Don't you worry about the serpent. I have a punishment ready for him, but that doesn't let you two off the hook.

ADAM: But it wasn't my fault; she made me do it.

EVE: Ooh, you spineless fibber.

ADAM: I am not spineless.

EVE: Yes you are.

ADAM: Am not.

EVE: Are too.

ADAM: Am not.

EVE: Are too.

Short fight sequence with Laurel and Hardy-style single

choreographed movements. For instance, ear twisting,
knuckle crunching, eye poking, toe stamping and face slapping.

GOD: Children, children! CHILDREN! (*They stop*) Look at
me. (*ADAM and EVE look, face front, stock still*)
You were my first two children, whom I adored
above all creation. For you I made this idyllic garden
and I delighted to see you enjoy it. I wanted to give
you immortal life, in this paradise of Eden, but you
disobeyed me, and worse still you tried to hide your
disobedience from me, as if that were possible. Your
punishment then: expulsion from the Garden of
Eden. Never again will you return to this paradise.

ADAM: (*Pause*) But . . . God. . . .

EVE: He's gone.

ADAM: Well, this is a right pickle you've got us in.

EVE: Me!

ADAM: Yes, you! I told you that serpent was a bit iffy.

EVE: Oh that's easy to say now.

ADAM: And what was all that about, hiding an apple from
the Lord of all creation behind your back! (*Mimics
EVE hiding apple*) 'Ooh, where did that come from?'
Pathetic!

EVE: Well, you can talk: (*Mimics ADAM whining*) 'But it
wasn't my fault, she made me do it!' Typical man!

ADAM: What do you mean 'typical man'? I'm the only man!

EVE: Exactly! . . . Look, let's stop arguing, eh? It's just
about doing my head in.

ADAM: Yeah . . . (*Pause*) I'm really gonna miss this place.

EVE: Me too. Come on, we'd better go and pack our bags.
(*EVE exits*)

ADAM: (*Confused pause*) Pack our bags! We haven't got
anything. (*He sees an apple core, picks it up, pauses*

*for thought then throws it away. ADAM exits. Fade
to blackout*)

TEACHING POINT

Hiding our sin from God is futile.

BIBLE REFERENCE

Proverbs 28:13

Hubrasixtus Fallycrygenic

A gossip betrays a confidence; so avoid a man who talks too much.

INTRODUCTION

When I studied Proverbs to find ideas for themes of sketches in this book, one I felt I couldn't overlook was gossiping. Somehow, the temptation to gossip is intrinsic to human nature – what better way to get an embarrassed laugh of recognition from an audience?

The performances should be bold and animated and, depending on the availability of actors, males could easily play female parts. (This also makes the subtle point that men are as good at gossiping as women.) The few speaking parts should be supported by a number of extras as patients in the waiting room – as many as possible, depending on your resources.

Characters: MARINA, KATHY, HENRY, SYLVIA. Plus a group of non-speaking extras.

To open the sketch, the cast should create a rhythmic sound of coughing, sneezing and general sounds of aches and pains. The lights come up on the doctor's waiting room; HENRY and KATHY are already waiting with other patients; SYLVIA is off stage with the doctor; MARINA enters dressed for winter; she stamps the snow off her boots three times, at which point the rhythm ends.

MARINA: Ooh, you could catch your death of pneumonia out
there today, couldn't you?

KATHY: That you could, my love, that you could. Here, take the weight off.

MARINA: Oh, thanks ever so. (*She sits*) By the way, my name's Marina.

KATHY: Oh, Kathy, nice to meet you.

MARINA: You too. Behind as usual, are they?

KATHY: Of course. What do you expect from the NHS nowadays?

MARINA: I know; it beggars belief doesn't it? You know who I blame.

KATHY: No, who?

MARINA: That Jeffrey Archer.

KATHY: (*Surprised*) Jeffrey Archer! Why d'ya blame him?

MARINA: I don't know. I just can't stand his guts, so I blame him for everything.

KATHY: Oh, I see.

MARINA: Mind you, that *Kane and Abel* weren't bad on TV, though, I suppose.

KATHY: Mmm.

MARINA: (*Picks up newspaper from table*) So, what's happening in the world today then?

KATHY: Ooh they're all out of date, Marina love; I had a look earlier.

MARINA: Let's see. (*Reading out loud*) John Lennon shot dead. Oh dear, oh dear, oh dear. Why do I pay my stamp?

KATHY: Mind you, that last woman's been in there so long, maybe I have been sitting here 20 years.

MARINA: (*Digging through magazines*) Good grief, what about this one! *Woman's Own*, Queen's Silver Jubilee Special. It beggars belief.

HENRY: (*Bursts into a fit of coughing*)

MARINA: Are you quite all right?

HENRY: Not too bad, love, thanks.

MARINA: Well, I wouldn't be too optimistic if I were you;
that sounded like a chronic death rattle to me.
Wouldn't you agree, Kathleen?

KATHY: Mmm. I must admit it didn't sound too healthy.

HENRY: I'm fine, ladies; don't worry yourselves.

MARINA: I'm not worried, unless it's catching. It's not, is it?

HENRY: No, nothing like that.

MARINA: Smoker, are you?

HENRY: Yes, I am, as a matter of fact.

MARINA: (*Tuts*) Well what do you expect? Not that I'm
being judgemental or anything. No, that's not my
style. . . . I do find it rather annoying though, having to wait to see the doctor with a justified ail-
ment just because people like you are daft enough
to smoke yourself into an early grave.

KATHY: Here here.

HENRY: If you must know, this is just a winter cold. It hasn't
got the slightest thing to do with my being here.

MARINA: Oh well, excuse me. (*Pause*) So, er, why *are* you
here then?

HENRY: Well, it's a little bit personal if you don't mind.

MARINA: Oh, I see. I'll take it no further then.

HENRY: Thank you, if you wouldn't mind.

MARINA: (*Pause*) Waterworks problems, is it?

HENRY: NO! There's nothing wrong with my waterworks,
thank you very much. They're all flowing wonderfully well.

KATHY: Well, of course that can sometimes be the problem
with them. They're flowing so well you can't get
them to stop!

HENRY: That may be so, but not in my case. They flow
when I want them to flow; they desist when I want

them to desist. Now, if you don't mind.

MARINA: Of course, in a man of your age, problems with the prostate gland are very commonplace.

HENRY: (*Annoyed*) There's nothing wrong with my prostate gland!! (*Calms down*) Look, if you really must know why I'm here ... Well, look, you promise you won't tell a soul?

MARINA: Oh, you have my absolute word of honour; my lips are sealed.

KATHY: Me too. We'll just keep it between the three of us.

HENRY: Well, I'm suffering from a condition called Hubrasixtus Fallycrygenic.

MARINA: (*Shock*) Not Hubrasixtus Fallycrygenic! What's that then?

KATHY: No idea.

MARINA: So what's that then?

HENRY: Well, it's a tad embarrassing really but ... look, you really won't tell another soul?

MARINA: Cross my heart, hope to die, stick a needle through my eye. I can't say fairer than that.

HENRY: Well it's ... (*He leans over to whisper. KATHY and MARINA give suitable shocked reactions*)

OFF STAGE: Next patient, please. (*SYLVIA hobbles on stage with two walking sticks, HENRY gets up to go and see doctor*)

HENRY: That's me; see you, ladies. (*HENRY exits*)

KATHY: Bye bye.

MARINA: Yeah, ta ta.

SYLVIA: (*Heading to HENRY'S seat*) Is this seat taken, dear?

MARINA: No ... Yes, no, I mean don't sit there. (*MARINA removes chair with fingertips, and gets another one for SYLVIA. SYLVIA is now seated between MARINA and KATHY*)

SYLVIA: Thank you, dear. So what was wrong with that chair then?

MARINA: Well, let's just say that the man who was sitting there before has got a few problems. I can't say any more. We've been sworn to secrecy, haven't we Kathy?

KATHY: We certainly have, Marina.

MARINA: Frankly, it would be unethical of me to say any more.

KATHY: Well, it would be a betrayal in every sense of the word.

MARINA: Indeed it would. Harmful and unnecessary tittle-tattle.

KATHY: We built up a kind of confessional trust with him, didn't we.

MARINA: (*Turns on SYLVIA*) Yes, and to be honest, I think it's highly improper of you to keep digging for information!

SYLVIA: (*Innocently*) Well, I. . . .

MARINA: (*Interrupts*) But as it's you, and if you promise not to tell a soul, we'll make an exception.

SYLVIA: But you've no idea who I am.

MARINA: No, but you've got an honest face.

SYLVIA: Well, thank you.

KATHY: So, do you want to know or not?

MARINA: Of course she does, don't you?

SYLVIA: Well. . . .

MARINA: (*Interrupts*) Okay, if you insist, we'll tell you. He's got Hubrasixtus Fallycrygenic.

SYLVIA: What!

MARINA: I know, and I think it's highly contagious. I was only sitting next to him for five minutes, and every inch of my body has been itching ever since.

KATHY: The more I think about this, Marina, I believe it's our duty to tell everybody else. I mean, I don't think I could live with myself if there was an outbreak of Hubrasixtus Fallycrygenic on my conscience.

MARINA: You're right, Kathleen, you're so right. (*To waiting room in general*) Here, psst. Everybody. PSSSTT! (*Gets everyone's attention*) Gather around – I've got a very important announcement to make. Come on, come on, hurry up. (*Everyone clusters into a big circle*) Now before I start, you must all promise not to tell a soul, but, well . . . (*MARINA starts an audible animated whisper. We hear odd words, and see lots of exaggerated actions, along with various sighs and gasps from the group*) Now, remember what I said – don't tell a soul. (*As she says this HENRY re-enters*)

HENRY: Hello everyone. (*Group gives a shocked gasp and freezes.*)

MARINA: Oh, hello again.

HENRY: You haven't been, erm . . . ?

MARINA: Me! No! My lips are sealed (*Freeze and fade to blackout*)

TEACHING POINT

Spiritual Warning: gossips and gossiping can seriously damage your health.

BIBLE REFERENCE

Proverbs 20:19

Invite for Drinks

*A gentle answer turns away wrath, but a harsh word
stirs up anger.*

INTRODUCTION

The sketch, split into two halves, looks at the different out-
comes of a typical social situation. The message is that gentle
rather than harsh words make life more pleasant.

Characters: PETE, JANE.

*No set is required at all for this piece, unless you decide to
use a couple of chairs. In the first section PETE and JANE
are confrontational; in the second they are friendly and light
humoured. PETE and JANE walk on stage and freeze in their
opening positions. A short piece of music ends abruptly, and
the action begins.*

PETE: YOU'VE DONE WHAT?!
JANE: Calm down, Peter. There's good news and bad news. I
      just thought it would be nice for us to go round for
      drinks.
PETE: Round for drinks.
JANE: Yes.
PETE: With Maureen 'motormouth' Lever?
JANE: Yes.
PETE: Meaning I'll be stuck all night with dreary Derek!
JANE: Oh Peter, don't exaggerate. Derek isn't dreary.
PETE: Derek isn't dreary! If you look up dreary in the dic-
      tionary, there's a picture of Derek looking up at you.

(*Pulls a face*)

JANE: Now you're being silly.

PETE: Me silly! He collects and logs bus registration plates for goodness' sake. That's hardly the behaviour of a sane person.

JANE: How do you know that?

PETE: You were with us, Jane! Remember when we went for that meal at Latino's. He never cracked a smile all night, until that spanking new bus went by ... I've never seen him move so fast, chasing down North Street, notebook and pen in hand.

JANE: Well, anyway, you're not exactly Mr Exciting yourself.

PETE: I beg your pardon!

JANE: Moaning about him collecting bus numbers, you're a bit of a saddo collection freak yourself, aren't you?

PETE: And what would you be referring to?

JANE: Oh what do you think?

PETE: (*Pause*) If, my darling, you mean my complete collection of *Star Trek* videos, I'll have you know that's an investment!

JANE: Yeah, I'm sure there's crowds of people banging down the door to offer you thousands of pounds for them!

PETE: There's no need for sarcasm, Jane. Anyway, hang on a minute, you said there was good news and bad news.

JANE: Oh yeah.

PETE: So what's the good news?

JANE: That is the good news.

PETE: (*Look of shock*) What! Drinks with Maureen and Derek is the good news! Oh, no. What's the bad news?

JANE: (*Sheepishly*) Well, I don't know how to put it. I've had a little accident ... with your scale model of the starship *Enterprise*.

PETE gives an animated gasp; they freeze. There is another burst of music during which the freeze is broken and PETE and JANE retake their opening positions. The music ends and the action restarts.

PETE: So what have you arranged then?

JANE: We're just going round for a few drinks.

PETE: Round for drinks?

JANE: Yes.

PETE: With Maureen and Derek?

JANE: Yes. You don't mind, do you?

PETE: (*Pause, gives JANE a knowing look*) No, I suppose not . . . (*Points finger*) On condition that Derek doesn't start talking bus numbers!

JANE: (*Grabs PETE'S finger jokingly*) Well anything's better than conversation about *Star Trek*!

PETE: (*Mock indignation*) Ooh! Very quick witted today, aren't we? (*Affectionate tussle*) Gis a cuddle.

JANE: Do you know what? You're wonderful, you are!

PETE: (*Suspicious*) Hello, what are you after?

JANE: Nothing.

PETE: All right then, what have you done?

JANE: (*Guilty*) Nothing. (*Pause*) Well, I have got a teensy weensy confession.

PETE: Mmm?

JANE: Well . . . I was just dusting off the bookshelf in the spare room and . . . well, the complete works of William Shakespeare inadvertently fell . . .

PETE: Mmm?

JANE: . . . and landed on your scale model of the starship *Enterprise*.

PETE: (*A look of horror grows on his face*) You know, I never did like Shakespeare.

JANE: I'm really sorry.

PETE: Oh well, I'm sure it's nothing Scotty can't repair with a spot of superglue. (*Attempts impression of Scotty from* Star Trek) 'Captain, I don't think I have the capabilities.' (*They both laugh*)

JANE: You're so understanding.

PETE: Yeah, well you know what they say: (*They move to a position depicting a blissfully happy married couple and look at the audience*) a gentle answer turns away wrath, but harsh words cause quarrels.

They freeze as we hear closing bars of slushy music. Lights fade to blackout.

TEACHING POINT

Responding with gentle and kind words calms most situations. Harsh words inevitably cause rows.

BIBLE REFERENCE

Proverbs 15:1

It Takes Two to Tango

He who answers before listening – that is his folly and his shame.

INTRODUCTION

One of the most frustrating human traits is simply not to listen to what someone is saying to us. At best this can be annoying or rude, at worst it can cause the breakdown of a relationship. Based on Proverbs 18:13, this sketch looks at a mother's reaction to her daughter's announcement that she is pregnant. Although the confusion and family situation at the beginning of the sketch are comical, to illustrate the shame spoken of in the second half of the proverb, the piece ends rather darkly. The actors must carefully create this change of mood.

As you read the sketch, you will notice that the daughter concerned is Mary, the mother of Christ, and to this end the sketch could also be used at Christmas. I have used a lot of dramatic licence in the piece, as we don't know much about Mary's family life; her Aunt Elizabeth is mentioned of course! The setting is modern, and I've imagined just one scenario to humanise the story.

Characters: PAT, CLIVE, MARY.

Lights come up on CLIVE who is sitting at a table, reading the newspaper. PAT enters reading a letter.

PAT: Oh Clive, isn't it wonderful! I've had a lovely letter from my sister Elizabeth.

CLIVE: (*Uninterested*) Oh how spiffing!

71

PAT: Don't be like that. You like Elizabeth, don't you?

CLIVE: Well. . . .

PAT: Don't be silly; of course you do.

CLIVE: Anything you say, dear.

PAT: Anyway, I've invited her over to stay for a while.

CLIVE: Oh no! What the dickens made you do that, Pat?

PAT: You know full well why. What with her having a lit-
          tle bun in the oven, and Zach away with work for the
          next couple of weeks, I thought she might need my
          sisterly support.

CLIVE: I thought you didn't agree with her having this baby.

PAT: Well, no I admit it. I think at her age she's a bit past
          childbearing – I mean she's no spring chicken, is she?

CLIVE: She's younger than you are!

PAT: SHUT IT! Anyway, I just think that at times like this
          family should draw together, so that's why I invited
          her. Misery guts!

CLIVE: So, what does she say in this here letter then?

PAT: Well, bless her, she says . . . (*Reads letter*) 'I really
          don't want to get in the way and be a trial for you
          and Clive, so I don't think I should come.'

CLIVE: Oh good!

PAT: 'But if it makes you feel better, Pat, I'll come
          straight over.'

CLIVE: Oh blimey, all the peace in this house will be shat-
          tered.

PAT: Oh stop moaning and read your paper.
          (*MARY enters looking nervous*)

PAT: Hello, love. Ooh you look like you've seen a ghost.
          Sit down and have a cuppa, for goodness' sake!

MARY: Thanks.

CLIVE: You sure you're all right, love?

PAT: Course she is, Clive. Now stop interfering. (*CLIVE throws up arms in despair and continues reading newspaper*) Out till all hours with your boyfriend last night, were you?

MARY: He has got a name, Mum, and he's not my boyfriend, he's my fiancé actually.

PAT: Oh excuse me. I keep forgetting he's your betrothed. (*Nudges MARY*) Ooh, your dad's been getting all excited. Auntie Elizabeth's coming to stay. (*CLIVE has a look of dread*)

MARY: Oh that's handy, I was going to go and see her later.

PAT: Oh yeah, why was that, love?

MARY: (*Stuttering*) Oh . . . erm . . . Well, nothing in particular; just to see how she was.

PAT: Oh, what a good girl you are. Better than some husbands I could mention. . . . Ooh it's so exciting: I'm going to be an auntie.

MARY: And a grand. . . . (*Stops herself*)

PAT: What was that, love?

MARY: And a gr . . . and a gr . . . grand auntie you'll make too.

PAT: Ahhh, thank you, love. Isn't that sweet, Clive?

CLIVE: Mmm?

PAT: Oh forget it. . . . Are you sure you're all right, Mary love?

MARY: I'm not really sure how to feel. Look, Mum, Dad, I've got something really big to tell you.

PAT: (*Unsure*) Oh yeah?

MARY: I think it might come as, well, rather a shock.

CLIVE: This is all beginning to sound rather ominous.

PAT: Be quiet, Clive.

MARY: Well . . . I'm pregnant.

PAT: (*Pause*) No, you're all confused, love. That's your Aunt Elizabeth. You're just a teenager, a kid.

MARY: I know it's hard to take in, but it's true. I am pregnant.

PAT: You ... you ... you stupid girl! How could you be so, so STUPID!

MARY: Listen Mum ...

PAT: (*Cuts in*) Don't 'listen Mum' me.

CLIVE: Are you 100 per cent sure, love?

PAT: Oh don't interfere, Clive; this is nothing to do with you.

MARY: Mum!

PAT: Well, are you 100 per cent sure then?

MARY: Yes. I've done one of those kits, but I'd had it on the highest authority anyway.

PAT: Oh Mary, why did you do it? This isn't how I brought you up, is it? I taught you to be God-fearing and full of morals. I gave you so many morals you had them coming out your ears.

MARY: But Mum ...

PAT: Don't stop me midflow, Mary. It's my duty as a loving mother to give you a lecture, so sit back and listen.

MARY: But you don't understand. . . .

PAT: Oh, I think I do. I'm a wise woman of the world. I know the facts of life, Mary, and I know how these little mistakes happen. You young people, you've got no respect, no idea of standards. Look at your father. Look, you've broken his heart, hasn't she Clive?

CLIVE: Well ...

PAT: (*Interrupts*) See! Speechless he is. Rendered totally speechless by your stupidity.

MARY: Please listen to me.

PAT: Of course I blame your Aunt Elizabeth. It's her, with her getting up the duff at her age; she's put silly ideas into your head.

MARY: No Mum.

PAT: Ooh, you wait till she gets here. I'll have it out with her. I'd got a Sara Lee gateau in especially for her too; there's gratitude for you.

CLIVE: Look, maybe we should . . .

PAT: Keep your nose out, Clive! If you can't say anything useful, it's best to say nothing at all. (*Pause*) So, I suppose you'll expect me to look after the baby?

MARY: No.

PAT: Oh I can see it now. Granny with the sprog, up to her armpits in ploppy nappies, while you go gadding off nightclubbing with your boyfriend.

MARY: Fiancé!

PAT: Engaged you may be, but you're supposed to wait until you get married. Ooh, you wait till I see his mum; she'll roast him over the coals when she gets her hands on him.

MARY: It's not Joe's fault anyway.

PAT: Not Joe's fault! Oh, did you hear that, Clive?

CLIVE: Yeah.

PAT: Not his fault my foot. I'm not letting you off the hook, but just remember it takes two to tango.

CLIVE: Doing the tango doesn't get you pregnant, love.

PAT: Clive, do us all a favour and give your jaw a rest. Anyway, if Joe decided he couldn't wait to tango, couldn't he have at least taken certain precautions?

MARY: Mum, we didn't tango.

PAT: Oh don't you start too; it's bad enough with your father.

MARY: Why can't you just listen to me? Joe isn't the father! (*Stunned silence and looks of horror*)

PAT: But . . . I . . . th . . . he . . .

CLIVE: I think what your mother is trying to say is, if it's not Joe, who is it?

MARY: (*Pause*) I think I'd better save that for another day.

PAT: You're dirty, Mary. You don't deserve to live under this roof, be part of this family. I wish, I wish I'd never had you.

MARY: (*Upset*) Mum, please don't say that.

CLIVE: Pat, stop it.

PAT: Shut up! I'll say my piece. My daughter the neighbourhood good-time girl – we'll be the laughing stock. This is not how it should be. This is not how I meant it to be. Oh, go and run off and see your Aunt Elizabeth.

MARY: I will.

CLIVE: Mary, I . . . (*He can't find the words*)

MARY: You'll never understand, Mum, because you never listen. What I've been trying to tell you all along is . . . I'm still a virgin. (*Suitable expressions of shock and confusion; lights fade to blackout*)

TEACHING POINT

If we fail to listen properly, we can end up with a serious amount of egg on our faces.

BIBLE REFERENCE

Proverbs 18:13

Leaning on MOU

Trust in the LORD with all your heart and lean not on your own understanding.

INTRODUCTION

Based on one of the most famous proverbs, this sketch is a silly but visual illustration of the dangers of relying too much on ourselves and not enough on the Lord. The actor playing THREE should be as big as possible! Acting ability need not be high as he utters a few words only, but a large physical presence in bouncer-style costume will add greatly to the effect of the sketch.

The piece ends with an a cappella song. PLEASE do not be put off by this, as it is relatively easy to put together a slick finale.

Characters: ONE, TWO, THREE.

Lights come up on TWO, who is asleep and leaning on THREE, who is standing like a bouncer with suit and sunglasses. THREE also has a sign around him which has in bold letters. 'MOU'. ONE enters, looks confused, and attempts to wake up TWO.

ONE: Excuse me. Excuse me!

TWO: (*Stumbles*) AGGHHH! Ooh, you gave me a fright.

ONE: Sorry, I just. . . .

TWO: Sorry! Sorry he says, d'ya hear that?

THREE: Yeah!

TWO: Well, sorry's not good enough, matey. You'll end up giving someone a coronary, creeping up on them, yelling down their lughole.

ONE: Well, I don't make a habit of it! I just thought you might have keeled over or something.

TWO: Any more of your shock tactics and I probably will. Would you credit some people, eh?

THREE: Nah!

TWO: Just trying to get a few moments of peaceful shut-eye, and they assume you must be dead!

ONE: Well, you must admit it is a bit strange.

TWO: What?

ONE: Well, this.

TWO: WHAT?

ONE: You standing in the middle of the street, leaning against . . . him!

TWO: Well, I don't see what's so strange in all that. Do you see what's so strange in all that?

THREE: Nah!

TWO: See. That's two against one. You must be the strange one.

ONE: Oh come off it, it's not something you see every day, is it?

TWO: Not something you see everyday, he says. Tut tut tut!

THREE: Tut tut tut!

TWO: It's a lot more common than you think, pal.

ONE: What is?

TWO: Oh blimey! What a goon brain.

ONE: Come on then, tell me.

TWO: Well, I can't see that it's any of your business really.

ONE: Oh go on.

TWO: (*Pause*) What do you think? Should I tell him?

THREE: (*Sharp intake of breath*) Yeah!

TWO: All right then. I've forgotten the question now.

ONE: Oh, for goodness' sake, WHAT ARE YOU DOING?

TWO: Oh yeah, that's right. Now, how shall I put it? Erm. Leaning.

ONE: Leaning.

TWO: Yep, that's right. Leaning.

ONE: Why?

TWO: Free country, isn't it?

ONE: Well I suppose so, but what exactly is it you're leaning on?

TWO: (*Points at THREE*) What that?

ONE: Yes.

TWO: You want to know what that is that I'm leaning on?

ONE: Yes.

TWO: Did you hear him? He wants to know what I'm leaning on.

THREE: Yeah!

TWO: Well if you must know, Mr Nosey Parker, it's my own understanding.

ONE: Eh?

TWO: Oh give me strength. (*Points slowly at letters on sign*) My Own Understanding.

ONE: (*Pause*) So, let me get this straight. You're leaning on your own understanding?

TWO: Bingo! He's quick this boy; give him credit.

ONE: Isn't that a bit dangerous?

TWO: Why?

ONE: Well, what happens if your own understanding lets you down?

TWO: Calm down, boy, calm down. Blimey, if you're not careful you'll set him off. He doesn't take too kindly to the suggestion that he's fallible.

ONE: Look, I don't want to be offensive, but surely he is. Your own understanding can't possibly know everything.

TWO: Are you saying he's a thicko?

ONE: No, of course not. Just that maybe it would be wiser to lean elsewhere for your support.

TWO: Look, if you don't believe me, test him.

ONE: What?

TWO: Test him. Any question you like – I think you'll be amazed.

ONE: Well, that's not really the point.

TWO: Come on, chicken, you started this.

ONE: Okay, okay! All right, what's the capital of France?

THREE: Paris.

TWO: Too easy, come on! Think of something hard.

ONE: Erm . . . how about this one? Who wrote *Uncle Vanya*?

THREE: Chekhov.

TWO: Easy peasy lemon squeezy! These are mildly offensive: come on, a proper test.

ONE: Well, I think I'll get you with this one. What is the square root of 9409?

THREE: Ninety-seven.

TWO: Impressive, isn't he?

ONE: Very.

TWO: So maybe leaning on your own understanding is okay after all.

ONE: Well, maybe . . . to a point.

TWO: To a point; listen to him.

ONE: How about one more question?

TWO: Go on then, fire away.

ONE: How can your own understanding make your paths straight?

THREE: (*Pause, jerks*) Malfunction.

TWO: Woo, take it easy.

ONE: Oh, not so good on that one was he? How about a nice wildlife question? How can a camel pass through the eye of a needle?

THREE: (*Jerks wildly, TWO holds on*) System overload warning!

TWO: Okay, point taken. Maybe certain things are a tad beyond my own understanding.

ONE: Ah good, you're seeing reason at last. Just one final question. How many hairs do you have on your head?

THREE: System failure. (*THREE moves and TWO falls to the floor*)

TWO: Agh! Ooh that's my hip, you big hopeless lunkhead. That's the last time I lean on you.

ONE: Ah the message has finally got through.

TWO: Ooh, don't you just hate a smarmy winner? Come on then, clever clogs, share with us all the moral of this tale.

ONE: Well, it's very simple.

To end the sketch the three actors perform an a cappella version of 'Lean on me', changing the words to 'Lean on the Lord'. This is not as difficult as it sounds and you need only do a short clip from the chorus. Use finger clicking and leg slapping to establish the rhythm and vocal sounds for a beat box and the tune. For comic effect use THREE to hit some really low notes and the strongest singer should sing the words.

TEACHING POINT

Do not lean solely on your own understanding, but put your trust in the Lord.

BIBLE REFERENCE

Proverbs 3:5–6

The Legend of Nottingham Forest

A simple man believes anything, but a prudent man gives thought to his steps.

INTRODUCTION

How is it that people accept legends like Robin Hood as fact, but despite the overwhelming historical evidence about Jesus, still consider anything biblical as mere fairy stories? This sketch looks at belief and how the wise respond to facts. Proverbs 14:15 shows us that while the fool believes anything put before him, the wise person prudently checks out the facts first. The Bloggs family used in *50 Sketches About Jesus* return to illustrate this point. They require strong character performances.

Characters: MR BLOGGS, MRS BLOGGS, MASTER BLOGGS, MISS BLOGGS.

MR BLOGGS and MRS BLOGGS are sitting centre stage. Loud music off stage increasingly infuriates MR BLOGGS.

MR: Turn that racket down, Miss Bloggs; it's doing my brain in! (*Music gets louder*) Sort her out, Mrs Bloggs, or I swear I'll go up and swing for her!

MRS: (*Stands to call up stairs*) Miss Bloggs, turn it down please. We can't hear ourselves think down here. Put your new headphones on or something. Oh, I give up.

MR: (*Stands defiantly*) Right, I'm gonna go up there and brain her. (*Music stops suddenly. Pause of dis-*

	belief) Ahhh, bliss!
MASTER:	(*Enters*) Hi ya.
MRS:	Hello, Master Bloggs.
MR:	Ooh, he's back at last. Where have you been gadding off to then?
MASTER:	Just down the shops.
MR:	(*Annoyingly*) Wiv yer girlfriend?
MRS:	Mr Bloggs!
MR:	What! I'm only asking . . . Come on then, Master Bloggs, what was it, birds or mates?
MASTER:	It was a mixed group if you must know.
MR:	Woo hoo!! Mixed eh? Anyone special we should know about?
MASTER:	No!
MRS:	Leave it be, Mr Bloggs.
MR:	I dunno, you can't even ask about your family's well-being in this place.
MISS:	(*Enters with headphones on, singing*)
MR:	Oh blimey.
MISS:	Wanna have a listen, Mr Bloggs?
MR:	I'd rather shove my ears in a blender!
MISS:	Oh sorry, I forgot you only like trendy rock 'n' roll.
MR:	(*Defensive*) Eh! There's nothing wrong with rock 'n' roll. Better than all that boom boom boom racket! Do us all a turn and switch it off for a bit.
MISS:	(*Turns off stereo and sits down*) What's on the box tonight then?
MRS:	I'm just having a look.
MR:	I wouldn't bother, Mrs Bloggs. It's bound to be a load of old tripe as usual.
MISS:	That don't stop you watching it twelve hours a day.

MR: Oh very tactful, Miss Bloggs: you know it's a medical condition that confines me to my chair for most of the day.

MISS: Yeah, lazyitus!

MRS: That's enough from you. Now, they've got that film *Robin Hood Prince of Thieves* on at ten past eight.

MR: Oh, I hate him.

MISS: Who, Robin Hood?

MR: No! You can't hate Robin Hood: he's a national hero. I mean, I hate that Kevin Costner.

MRS: Ooh, I think he's gorgeous.

MR: Yeah, you would! You fancy anything in a pair of jodhpurs.

MASTER: How do you figure that Robin Hood's a national hero then?

MR: Eh? Well, he was a few hundred years ago, weren't he? It's fact. Robbing from the rich, giving to the poor – little bit like an early Tony Blair. You could do well to watch it, Miss Bloggs – learn a little bit about history.

MISS: Oh I hate historical drama. What's on the other side?

MASTER: I'm sorry to disappoint you all, but Robin Hood isn't actually an historical figure: he's just a legend, possibly loosely based on some facts.

MR: Don't be so daft, Master Bloggs. 'Course he's real. If you'd gone up to Nottingham Forest a few centuries ago you'd have seen him yourself, cavorting round with his bows and arrows. Now you just see the football team get stuffed twice a week!

MISS: It's not Nottingham Forest, Mr Bloggs, it's Sherwood Forest.

MR: Yeah, whatever, and then there's his bit of stuff Maid wotsername, and that big, fat, greedy monk.

MRS: Maid Marian and Friar Tuck.

MR: Exactly, case proved, Master Bloggs.

MASTER: Just because there's a Sherwood Forest, it doesn't automatically follow that there's a Robin Hood.

MISS: What do you mean?

MASTER: Well, we've got a chimney, but it don't mean that Father Christmas comes scooting down it every year.

MRS: (*Upset*) Don't he?

MR: Shut up, Mrs Bloggs!

MISS: Anyway, you're a fine one to talk about myths and legends, Mr Christian – at least we don't believe in some airy fairy Jesus.

MR: She's got a fair point, Master Bloggs.

MASTER: Well, not really: there's loads of documented evidence about the existence of Jesus.

MISS: Yeah, if you believe the Bible.

MASTER: Not just in the Bible, in other historical works too. In fact, there's probably more written about the existence of Jesus than there is about figures such as Caesar or Cleopatra.

MR: Oh, so now you're saying that Caesar didn't exist!

MASTER: No, I'm merely making the point that any historian would certainly accept Jesus' existence, as they would do Caesar's, but most likely reject the historical accuracy of Robin Hood.

MRS: And what about Father Christmas?

MR: Oh will you shut up about Father Christmas, Mrs Bloggs!

MISS: Well, I still don't believe in no Jesus: I think it's all a load of rubbish.

MASTER: That's your choice, Miss Bloggs, but I think you're in the minority. So, are we gonna watch *Robin Hood Prince of Thieves* then?

MR: I thought you said it was a load of rubbish.

MASTER: Well, it's still a good film though, innit?

MR: Oh no! You've spoilt it now, saying it's a load of hocus-pocus. What's on the other side, Mrs Bloggs?

MRS: (*She is snivelling*)

MR: Oh stop snivelling, Mrs Bloggs; I've told you a thousand times Father Christmas is made up.

MRS: I know. . . .

MR: So, what's on the other channel?

MRS: (*Pulling herself together*) Um . . . oh *Gandhi*'s on in ten minutes.

MR: *Gandhi*! No, I don't fancy that.

MASTER: Why not?

MR: Well, it's much too far fetched.

MASTER: (*Buries head in hands in disbelief. Fade to black-out*)

TEACHING POINT

If you take the time to check the facts about Christianity, you will find that it makes sense!

BIBLE REFERENCE

Proverbs 14:15

Millennium Bug

There is surely a future hope for you, and your hope will not be cut off.

INTRODUCTION

This millennium-based sketch has a twist – it is set at the turn of the last millennium. I've often wondered what people were discussing about future aspirations then, and whether maybe they weren't too far off the things we discuss a thousand years on. The central theme of the piece is that our eternal future is in God's hands, no matter when we live.

Characters: MAN, WOMAN.

Lights go up on WOMAN sitting centre stage knitting.

MAN: (*Rushes in*) What do you think you're doing, woman?

WOMAN: Knitting. What does it look like, husband?

MAN: Knitting! How can you be knitting at a time like this?

WOMAN: Easy, watch. (*She continues to knit in an exaggerated fashion*)

MAN: Stop it, you daft baggage! (*He tries to grab knitting*)

WOMAN: LEAVE IT!! Oh, now look what you've made me do. I've dropped me pearl stitch, you great big lummox!

MAN: Big lummox am I? Here I am trying to protect my woman from I don't know what, as is my primal instinct, and all I get is a load of abuse.

WOMAN: Oh don't talk such rot.

MAN: (*Declaring*) As your husband I charge thee woman to put down thy knitting!

WOMAN: (*Pause*) Ooh, I love it when you get all masculine.

MAN: Just put it down!

WOMAN: Oh anything for a bit of peace and quiet I suppose.

MAN: Good, now lie face down and cover your ears. This could be loud.

WOMAN: What?

MAN: Hurry up, woman, we've less than a minute to go. (*She obeys reluctantly, and he lies beside her protectively*) 10–9–8–7–6–5–4–3–2–1–0. (*We hear distant celebrations off stage. MAN looks up cautiously and confused*)

WOMAN: Well, that was spectacular! Happy New Millennium, husband.

MAN: Maybe I've got the time wrong.

WOMAN: I don't think so. I can hear the rest of the street celebrating. I think you can safely say no longer is it the year 999 – we've safely arrived at the year 1000. A brand-new millennium.

MAN: What about all them soothsayers who have been giving it all that for the past century?

WOMAN: (*Imitating soothsayer*) 'Woe, woe! Beware the time is upon us when this world shall be no more. BEWARE!' Snaggle-toothed old hags.

MAN: But so many predicted the same thing. The earth would end at the stroke of midnight.

WOMAN: Well, they're all wrong!

MAN: Mind you, maybe the calendar's wrong.

WOMAN: What?

MAN: I heard a rumour that they've got the date wrong. The actual date of the official millennium is 1001.

WOMAN: Oh don't be so daft.

MAN: Losing count just once during all those centuries – it's easily done.

WOMAN: Well, if you think I'm going through all this malarkey again next year, you've got another think coming.

MAN: Yes, next year. That's got to be it. I mean, something's got to happen soon: look at the state the world's in!

WOMAN: It's not that bad. Mind you, I wish someone would hurry up and invent electricity.

MAN: Eh?

WOMAN: Well, it gets on my nerves stumbling around in the dark to go to the loo in the middle of the night. It's primitive!

MAN: Electricity! What are you talking about, woman?

WOMAN: And what about that Millennium Bug?

MAN: What about it?

WOMAN: Well, Mary two doors down has been laid up with it for the past fortnight. Nausea, vomiting, the lot!

MAN: Oh spare me the details.

WOMAN: Well, that bug I can do without.

MAN: Never fear my dear. A little Millennium Bug wouldn't stand a chance against you. You've got the constitution of an ox!

WOMAN: Oi, that's enough of your lip. (*He laughs*) You won't be laughing if I go down with something. Who'll be cooking your stew then?

MAN: I'm sorry, woman; it's just my little joke.

WOMAN: Well, that's quite enough of your jokes for the next millennium, thank you very much. Now, where's my knitting? (*She picks up knitting and continues*)

MAN: (*In deep thought*) 1000 AD, unbelievable innit?

Mind you, something will happen soon, mark my words.

WOMAN: Like what?

MAN: I dunno, but something will. All them prophecies can't be wrong, surely?

WOMAN: Oh don't start on about them again.

MAN: Well, it's all started to happen, hasn't it? We've got violence, wars, famine, poverty. Blimey, imagine what a total mess the planet will be in if it goes on for another thousand years.

WOMAN: 2000 AD. Very science fiction.

MAN: No, we'll never last that long.

WOMAN: Well, you won't, don't worry. You won't make it through this winter if I don't finish off this scarf for you sharpish.

MAN: 2000 AD. Well, if we do last that long at least there'll be a cure for that Millennium Bug.

WOMAN: (*Pause*) I wouldn't bet on it.

MAN: Eh?

WOMAN: Forget it; let's join in the celebrations.

MAN: Mmm, why not! (*He grabs her by the hand and they exit singing 'Auld Lang Syne'. Lights fade to blackout*)

TEACHING POINT

Throughout the ages people have pondered the future. Where does your hope for the future lie?

BIBLE REFERENCES

Proverbs 23:18; 24:14

Never-Never Land

*The rich rule over the poor, and the borrower is servant
to the lender.*

INTRODUCTION

At the time of writing this piece Britain and America had just
announced the cancellation of Third World debt, and were in
the process of lobbying other governments to follow suit.
Using the proverb relating to debt, my original thought had
been to write a piece on the Third World situation, but in the
light of recent events I changed my mind. Instead, I made the
subject an individual who has got himself caught in the
moneylending web. It has always interested me that in Old
Testament history, falling into debt was one of the worst sins
you could commit – yet today all of us have mortgages, car
loans or credit cards and view borrowing as normal. With so
many offers and companies throwing money at us, we must
discern what is acceptable and what is not.

The monologue should be played with moments of gentle
humour to glimpse the 'good old days', but in reality it por-
trays a man ruined by his debts.

Character: JOHN.

JOHN: It's taken me years to admit it, but looking back now I
reckon that sometimes, just maybe, I should have listened
to my old dad. He was a daft old duffer, no mistake, and
most of his so-called advice was, well, vaguely ludicrous.
For instance, his prehistoric opinion on how a man should
treat his woman was so frighteningly non-PC – to speak it

aloud in our enlightened times would very likely herald prosecution and an immediate lynch mob! But on the odd occasion – very seldom, I admit – he would come out with an absolute gem. Now, one of his overlooked classics – and I can hear him say the words now as if it were yesterday – was this: 'Never pay on the never-never. If you can't afford it, you can't have it.' Not startlingly original advice, I admit. Thousands of conservative parents have echoed this advice throughout the decades to errant and irresponsible offspring, but when I first heard these words of wisdom I was probably only about eleven or twelve, and the notion of being able to own something and never have to pay for it . . . well, it sounded pretty flipping amazing! Of course, I was to learn, by degrees, it doesn't quite work like that.

It wasn't very long before I had the opportunity to completely disregard Dad's advice on this particular point, when I secured my first job as a newspaper boy aged 13. I did two rounds, one in the morning and one in the evening, earning the princely sum of six pounds fifty pence a week. Now, Mr Jeffries, my employer, was a real shrewd businessman. Everyone thought he was dead shy and retiring but, I tell you, he never missed a trick that one. Anyway, as a special favour, only for his delivery boys and girls, he had this little black book, and we could run up a tab in advance of our wages on Saturday to buy sweets, comics, footy stickers or whatever. Well, I was in my element! My first introduction to buying things on the never-never. I would stuff sweets like they was going out of fashion, and Scrooge would carefully jot each transaction down in his little black book, watching his profits soar and my wages disappear. I remember one pay day I even owed him money, so my debt had to be carried on to the next week. I didn't care though:

in a funny way it seemed like it was all free 'cos I never saw the money in the first place. Looking back, I suppose that's where Jeffries was so clever.

I wish I could tell you that maturing into adulthood changed my ways, but it didn't. The lure of something for nothing or shortcut ways to live beyond my means has never lost its attraction. I'm the credit card company's original dream customer. 'Mr Paris, as a valued customer, blah blah blah, we would be delighted to extend your credit limit by a further thousand pounds.' I mean, how can you turn an offer like that down? When I got my first credit cards I had the express intent to pay them off in full at the end of each month – they were purely there for convenience I said to myself. Huh! Of course, in no time at all I was giving them the token minimum payment, convincing myself something would turn up next month so I could clear them. It wasn't just credit cards either. No! If only. Just about everything I owned was on the never-never. The new plush three-piece suite was no deposit, nothing to pay for a year with interest-free credit. Well, you can't go wrong, I thought. I got my Peugeot 306 1.9 injection on some super duper 3-2-1 special deal, with 36 low-cost monthly repayments. It all seemed so easy. The windows, cooker, washing machine, bedroom suite, shower unit – the whole lot – all on the never-never. I never went that mad: most of what I got was what you would call necessities. It's just that . . . well, I just wasn't that careful either. In the end I didn't know which way to turn; I was in a complete state, bills and demands all over the place. Then, out of the blue, an answer to my prayers. Or so I thought.

It dropped through the letter box with the post one morning, all colourful and inviting. A leaflet with a picture of a grinning has-been television presenter, all teeth and no brains. 'Pay off all your debts! Car, credit cards, the lot. We clear them all within 48 hours, leaving you with just one easy payment!' Fantastic! Only now I'm paying interest on top of the interest, and the longer it goes on, the worse it gets. The car was the first thing to go, then all the decent furniture, as you can see, and that's not to pay back what I borrowed, no – that's just to cover the mounting interest. When it gets to that state of affairs you really know you've blown it: you feel like a slave, worthless, but of course by then it's too late, much too late.

Which brings me to Julie, my wife. She moved out last week. Gone to live with her parents for a bit, temporarily like, or so she says. She can't cope any more, can't believe I didn't tell her what was happening, what a mess I'd got us into.   Where she thought the money was coming from I don't know, but we didn't discuss that; she just packed a few essentials and left. Another elegy from my dad that: 'The man controls the home finances, my son; it's got nothing to do with the woman: that's the way God intended it.'. . . (*Laughs to himself*) Soppy old duffer. So where do I go from here? Well, who knows? *Que sera sera,* so they say. Next month, right around the corner, something might just crop up. Wait and see. You never know. You never never know. (*He smiles, lights fade to blackout*)

TEACHING POINT

The importance of living within our own means, and not crippling ourselves with unaffordable debts.

BIBLE REFERENCE

Proverbs 22:7

Never Satisfied

A heart at peace gives life to the body, but envy rots the bones.

INTRODUCTION

Envy is one of the worst human traits. If we allow it to consume us, as the proverb so eloquently says, it can rot our bones. In this monologue, Maureen compares her life with that of her younger and more successful sister, Elizabeth. The more she tries to persuade herself and the listener otherwise, the more apparent it becomes that her envy towards Elizabeth controls her life. The monologue should be performed comically with a touch of pathos, and Maureen should be played with a degree of surfacing bitterness.

Character: MAUREEN.

The lights come up on MAUREEN, who is sitting at a table with a cup of tea and a slice of cake. She occasionally sips the tea and takes a bite of the cake.

MAUREEN: Personally I don't think it's fair that we always have to go round to hers. I mean, at the end of the day I am her older sister, and as such I think my opinion should count for something. She's done all right for herself, though, our Elizabeth. Married Charles, the merchant banker and they live in a lovely postmodernistic converted farmhouse on the outskirts of town. Don't get me wrong, though, I'm not envious or anything, no! It wouldn't be any good for us anyhow. Too much of that fresh country air

96

plays havoc with my Arthur's sinus condition – one whiff of cow dung and he's all bunged up for a fortnight.

'Maureen,' she says to me. 'Maureen, Charles and I are only too happy to jump in the Land-Rover or BM and come over to see you. We just thought you and Arthur might be more comfortable coming over to us. I can knock us up a lovely non-spicy something in the Aga, and then we can all eat out on the patio alfresco!' Alfresco, I ask you! 'And if Arthur wants a few cans of stout, you can always stay over in any one of our six spare bedrooms.' Flippin' cheek! She jolly well knows that Arthur's been off the stout for 18 months under doctor's orders due to his dodgy ticker. Arthur's always been one for the easy life, though, so we always go over there just to keep the peace. Liz gleefully shows us around all their new rooms and extensions. Ooh, you should see their new bathroom – twice the size of our lounge it is, and fully fitted with a bidet and all them new-fangled mod cons ... but, you know, she still sticks a bit of fluffy carpet on the toilet lid! It all stinks of the lower class-es who have made it good: breakfast bar, cloakroom, snooker lounge, conservatory, library – as if she ever reads! And we just nod and smile at all the appropriate times. Don't get me wrong, though, I'm not envious or anything, no! I'm very happy with our ex-council owned two up two down with its creaky staircase and outside loo, or should I say alfresco loo! I mean, it's a roof over your head, and that's all you need, isn't it? Mind you, it could do with a lick of paint, especially on the landing. There's not much chance of getting my Arthur up on a ladder nowadays, though; not after his quadruple hernia op. So, there you are – it'll just have to suffice, I suppose.

She phoned me up the other week, just before Wimbledon fortnight, all excited. 'Oh Maureen, you'll never guess what we've just bought.' A small country for all I know, I thought to myself, but I didn't say it out loud. 'A brand-new Nicam stereo, dolby surround, 3D phonic widescreen television. Charlie's going to set up an extension lead so I can watch Wimbledon alfresco on the verandah with champagne, strawberries and cream!' It's all right for some, isn't it, being able to drop the best part of a thousand pounds just like that for a new television set? Don't get me wrong, though, I'm not envious or anything, no! I'm perfectly happy with our Radio Rentals £49.99 ex-rental antique. Although I wouldn't say no to a remote control. Not for me, you understand: it's just not very good for Arthur getting up every five minutes to change the channel – not with his weak ankles. I honestly don't know why I fork out on a television licence any more. I mean, there's nothing on, is there, except a load of old repeats? To be frank, I don't watch a thing . . . well, except the soaps, and a bit of sport, but apart from that there's nothing! Although I'm not averse to a good murder mystery – not all of them, you understand. My preference is for *Morse* and *Frost*; well, they don't graphically show the murders, do they? *Changing Rooms*, *Ground Force*, *15 to 1*, *Countdown*, *Top of the Pops* . . . Ooh, and Des O'Connor, well, I never miss him; he's got such a lovely complexion, hasn't he? But apart from that, absolutely nothing. My Arthur always insists on the news. I find it so depressing; still, I suppose you need to keep up with the current issues, don't you? They had a report on the other evening – ooh it was ghastly, terrible. I don't know how these poor foreign people cope. I said to my Arthur, 'The whole thing's a criminal scandal.' He just grunted. Well, it's all he ever does do nowadays.

He's never been the same since he went to the hospital to have his prostate gland checked out. The doctor put his rubber glove on, asked Arthur to bend over, and well, he turned slate grey. He's not familiar with such intimacies. I said to him, 'It's lucky you're not a woman. A woman has to suffer invasions of privacy that would make your eyes water...even more than they did when the doctor . . . well, you know.' He just grunted.

The other thing Liz is getting all over-excited about is her upcoming hols. Apparently Saint Charles has booked them heaven on a stick: three weeks' cruising around the Caribbean on some luxury liner, followed by a couple of weeks' pampering at a five-star hotel. How smashing! I don't know how she'll manage to keep her posh accent up for five weeks. Don't get me wrong, though, I'm not envious or anything, no! I'm perfectly happy with two weeks at our usual holiday home in Camber Sands, complete with its leaking roof and psychotic maid. And anyway, it would be impossible for us to fly anywhere nowadays. Arthur's knees blow up like balloons if he goes above 10,000 feet: apparently it's water retention or some such thing. To be honest, though, I wouldn't say no to a change one year. Nothing abroad or anything flash like that; just somewhere nice – somewhere that you can sit out on your deckchair in peace without some infuriating little brat slamming a beach ball into your face every five minutes. Oh well, I suppose there's plenty a jolly sight worse off than me. Not that I'm complaining of course, no!

Well, I'm sure Liz and Charles will have an 'absolute ball'. She'll come back wearing a grin like a Cheshire cat, and with all that sun will no doubt be the colour of . . . well, the colour of a foreign person. And I'll tell you something else: she'll still want to go somewhere different, do something new, want something else. You see, that's the problem with rich people: they're never flippin' satisfied. What? What? (*MAUREEN has a bite from her cake and the lights slowly fade to blackout*)

TEACHING POINT

If you let any form of envy take root in your life, before you know it you will be consumed with bitterness.

BIBLE REFERENCE

Proverbs 14:30

The Noise the Unicorn Made

The mocker seeks wisdom and finds none, but knowledge comes easily to the discerning.

This sketch has to be the most surreal in the book, and for any avid theologians the centrality of a unicorn may seem somewhat suspect! However, during the writing stage of this collection, when I was reading sketches to a select audience, this one got more laughs than any other piece, so I had to include it.

While I was considering the theme in Proverbs of mocking and its consequences, I was drawn to the story of Noah, and how he was made the centre of mock and ridicule. The following piece is the result of that idea. You can make this work simply in a stylised way by having all the characters seated on stage, standing at the appropriate time to deliver their lines. The narrator holds the piece together and your strongest comic performer should play Ulysses the unicorn. Names can easily be amended to fit your male-to-female ratio of actors.

Characters: NARRATOR, NOAH, ULYSSES THE UNICORN, CARLA THE COW, DILYS THE DUCK.

All actors are seated on the stage, except the NARRATOR who is standing to one side.

NARR: Many, many moons ago, at the dawn of an early millennium, even before the invention of our calendar, there was a man and his name was Noah.

NOAH: How do you do; I'm building an ark and everyone thinks I'm a nutter!

NARR: God had personally asked Noah to build an ark and given him instructions to fill it with all manner of creatures: walking, crawling, slithering, waddling, flying and, rather strangely, swimming. So, ladies and gentlemen, for your delight and delectation, we have enlisted the help of some of the original characters, obviously now played by actors, to illustrate our story. Joining Noah . . .

NOAH: How do you do; I'm building an ark and everyone thinks I'm a nutter!

NARR: We have Carla the cow.

CARLA: Moo.

NARR: Dilys the duck.

DILYS: Quack.

NARR: And Ulysses the unicorn.

ULYSSES: (*He opens mouth to make noise, but looks puzzled*) Psst . . . Psst.

NARR: Mmm?

ULYSSES: What noise do I make?

NARR: I beg your pardon?

ULYSSES: What noise do I make?

NARR: Well, I don't know. You're the unicorn. Excuse us, ladies and gentlemen.

ULYSSES: That's as maybe, but I don't know what noise I'm supposed to make!

NARR: Well, just make one up for goodness' sake.

ULYSSES: Make one up!

NARR: Yes! Improvise. I'll cue you back in. Joining Noah whom you have already met.

NOAH: How do you do; I'm building an ark and everyone thinks I'm a nutter!

NARR: We have Carla the cow.

CARLA: Moo.

NARR: Dilys the duck.

DILYS: Quack.

NARR: And Ulysses the unicorn.

ULYSSES: (*Strange strangulated noise*)

NARR: (*Pause*) Is that the best you can do?

ULYSSES: If you can do any better be my guest.

NARR: All right, all right. I suppose it'll have to do. So, Noah's strange ark-building project, miles away from any water, was getting confused reactions from all the local neighbours.

CARLA: He's a nutter.

DILYS: He's a nutter.

ULYSSES: He's a nutter.

NOAH: Everyone thinks I'm a nutter!

NARR: But Noah was not to be discouraged: he was determined to fill the ark with all the creatures, just as God had instructed. He started his mission by meeting up with Carla the cow.

CARLA: Moo.

NOAH: How do you do; I'm building an ark and everyone thinks I'm a nutter!

CARLA: Well, Mr Noah, I'm hardly surprised. It does seem rather . . . well, rather doolally.

NOAH: Yes but there is a perfectly rational explanation.

NARR: Noah explained in great detail his obedience to God's plan and Carla listened with an open mind and great interest. (*During this speech NOAH mimes explanation to CARLA, complete with actions and the odd moo!*)

NOAH: And in addition to this, if you agree to join up today, I can still fix you up with one of the luxury upper-deck cabins with a sea view and access to the cocktail bars.

NARR: Carla the cow excitedly agreed.

CARLA: MOO!!

NARR: Noah's next customer, however, took a little more persuading. I suppose it was understandable for there to be some apprehension from Dilys the duck.

DILYS: Quack.

NOAH: Dilys, it is absolutely vital to the survival of your species that you agree to come aboard.

DILYS: Quack, why?

NOAH: Well, as I've been trying to explain to you for the past ten minutes, there's going to be the most dreadful flood. Towns, countries, continents, will be swept away. It's going to be a disaster of biblical proportions.

DILYS: Biblical? What's that then?

NOAH: You know biblical, as from the Bible.

DILYS: What's the Bible?

NOAH: Oh come on. You know. Oh, of course it's not been published yet, has it. Well, anyway it's going to be a disaster that's very bad.

DILYS: Look Noah, I don't mean any offence, but I just can't see what this whole thing's got to do with my family or me.

NOAH: Are you totally quackers? (*Looks to audience for sympathy*) Oh forget it; there's going to be a flood!

DILYS: So?

NOAH: So! What do you mean, 'So'?

DILYS: So, meaning, so what! It may have escaped your attention, Noah, and I don't want to appear ungrateful. But I can swim.

NOAH: (*Pause*) Oh, I see your point.

DILYS: Call me foolish, but a flood doesn't really fill me with dread as it might a human, cow (*CARLA moos*) or unicorn. (*ULYSSES makes noise*)

NOAH: Look, I know this might sound crazy, especially for you. I don't claim to understand it, but all I know is this ark will be the only refuge. Maybe the rain will be so torrential for so long, you won't physically be able to stand it; maybe the waters will become polluted. I don't know, but I do know that the ark will be the only escape. It's all too easy for you to mock me, but much harder for you to take a step of faith, Dilys. Now, I need to know: will you come?

NARR: Noah's heartfelt soliloquy sent a tear rolling down Dilys' beak, and she agreed to join Noah's band of intrepid sailors. A much tougher proposition was Ulysses the unicorn.

ULYSSES: (*Strangulated noise*) I've never heard of anything so utterly ridiculous in my life!

NOAH: What bit of it is so ridiculous?

ULYSSES: All of it! A flood that's going to wipe out life as we know it – it hardly seems likely, does it?

NOAH: It may seem unlikely, but I promise you it will happen.

ULYSSES: So you say. A dotty old crackpot with senile dementia. But of course the weather forecasters don't agree with you, do they?

NOAH: Well, they're never right. Look at that Michael Fish.

ULYSSES: Maybe, but that's not all. I mean, look at that ark.

NOAH: What about it?

ULYSSES: Well, it's not exactly the QE2, is it?

NOAH: It's been built to precise specifications, as instructed.

ULYSSES: Instructed by whom?

NOAH: God.

ULYSSES: God? What did he do, send you down a fax with the blueprint?

NOAH: No, not exactly . . . look, it's too complicated to explain, but if you don't come on board your whole species will be wiped out.

ULYSSES: Well, Noah, I'd love to come with you, I really would. But I know for a fact the Missis won't go for it.

NOAH: Can't you persuade her?

ULYSSES: If you knew Mrs Unicorn you'd know you can't persuade her about anything. No, she's very particular about her mode of transportation, and I don't think your rickety old ark will pass her stringent safety tests. Sorry, but what can I do?

NOAH: Well, if you change your mind, you know where to find me.

ULYSSES: With that monstrosity outside your house, everyone knows where to find you! (*He laughs*)

NOAH: Yes, well, cheerio Ulysses.

NARR: However hard Noah tried, he could do nothing to persuade Ulysses to come aboard the ark. The unicorn family mocked Noah and his fellow travellers and continued with their lives. Then, one day. . . .

NOAH: (*Holds out hand*) Hello, is that a drop of rain?

CARLA: (*Holds out hand*) Moo, is that a drop of rain?

DILYS: (*Holds out hand*) Quack, is that a drop of rain?

ULYSSES: (*Holds out hand, strangulated noise*) Oh bum!

NARR: It rained for 40 days and 40 nights and, as Noah had said, only the creatures aboard the ark survived the catastrophe. Carla the cow enjoyed her upper-deck cabin with sea views, and her species live to tell the tale.

CARLA: Moo.

NARR: As does Dilys the duck.

DILYS: Quack.

NARR: And Ulysses. . . . Well, to this day, no one really knows what noise the unicorn made.

ULYSSES: (*Strangulated noise; fade to blackout*)

TEACHING POINT

If you mock, are you prepared to shoulder the consequences?

BIBLE REFERENCE

Proverbs 14:6

Opposite Sides of a Coin

Stay away from a foolish man, for you will not find knowledge on his lips.

INTRODUCTION

King Solomon was a man who excelled in giving wise counsel, and Proverbs teaches us the import of doing the same. Although this sketch touches on the theme of sex, its central teaching is about how we choose whom to listen to, and the qualities we seek in our closest advisors. The piece should be played in a highly stylised way and no major movement is required. The three performers remain seated delivering their lines to the audience, except where there is dialogue.

Characters: ONE, TWO, THREE.

Lights come up on ONE, TWO and THREE who are all seated. ONE is in the middle and set slightly forward.

ONE: Why is life full of such dilemmas?
TWO: Well, it's all part of life's rich tapestry, isn't it.
ONE: If it's not one thing. . . .
THREE: You can bet your life it's something else.
ONE: I turn one way.
TWO: There's some looming catastrophe.
ONE: I turn the other way.
THREE: Life deals you yet another heffalump-sized body blow.
ONE: The car's cream crackered.
TWO: My hair looks like I've been dragged backwards

through a thorny bush.

THREE: The central heating system's making some dodgy rattling noise.

ONE: I've got so much cellulite it's spreading out to my fingertips!

TWO: My diet's gone right up the swanny.

THREE: And as usual. . . .

ALL: My bum looks huge in this!

ONE: Not to mention the complete bane of my life – MEN!

TWO: Blokes.

THREE: Geezers.

ONE: Up to all sorts as usual, and full of excuses.

TWO: (*As bloke*) 'Course I didn't forget your birthday, hun; it just temporarily slipped my mind.

THREE: (*As bloke*) I would have brought you flowers, babe, but I was right out of dosh.

TWO: (*As bloke*) I wasn't snogging that other bird, honest-ly. She started to faint so I had to give her mouth-to-mouth resuscitation!

ONE: And to win me over, they just had to look at me with those puppy-dog eyes, and say with apparent sincer-ity those immortal words. . . .

THREE: (*As bloke*) Babes, you know I love you.

ONE: Ooh, don't you just hate them?

ALL: (*Pause to look at one another*) No!

ONE: So, I had this guy on the go a while back, Dave was his name.

TWO: Painter and decorator.

THREE: Right cheeky chappie.

TWO: Fantastic body.

THREE: And a real eye for the ladies!

ONE: Anyway, we were out one night, celebrating our

two-week anniversary, and he gives me the speech.
You know the one.

TWO: (*As Dave*) Babes, we've been going steady for ages now, and I think we've reached the point in our relationship where it's time to . . . well, you know, move things on to a higher plateau, in a manner of speaking.

ONE: I understood perfectly where he was going with this, but for a laugh I thought I'd let him stumble on a bit longer.

THREE: (*As Dave*) Do you get my drift, babes? What I mean to say is, we can move things on a notch or two, in a more physical sense, if you know what I mean. You see I love you so much, I need to sort of explore other avenues to communicate in a more meaningful way the extent of my love for you, babes.

ONE: In plain English please, Dave!

TWO/THREE: (*Together*) Do you wanna have sex?

ONE: I admit Dave didn't have the romantic quality of a Shakespearian sonnet.

TWO: (*Over-the-top Shakespeare*) Romeo, Romeo. . . .

THREE: (*Over-the-top Shakespeare*) Wherefore art thou Romeo?

ONE: But I really fancied him, so I temporarily put him off, subject to a couple of essential girly chats.

TWO: This is where we come in.

THREE: And it all gets well juicy!

ONE: The only thing is, when you ask for a friend's counsel, on one hand . . .

TWO: You can get really good advice.

ONE: But on the other hand . . .

THREE: You can get really bad advice.

ONE: Bringing us back to the question: Why is life full of

such dilemmas? (*ONE and TWO turn to face each other, THREE freezes*)

TWO: What did you say his name was?

ONE: Dave.

TWO: And where did you meet him?

ONE: Cinderella's.

TWO: (*Sarcastic*) Ooh, very high class!

ONE: Don't joke, this is a serious situation.

TWO: Yeah I know, sorry.

ONE: So what should I do? What would you do?

TWO: Hang on, hang on. One question at a time.

ONE: Well, aren't they the same?

TWO: Look, I know what I would do, but at the end of the day that doesn't matter. The only thing that counts is what you're going to do, isn't it?

ONE: Yeah, I suppose.

TWO: So what are you going to do?

ONE: I don't know!

TWO: Well, how long have you known him?

ONE: Two weeks.

TWO: Two weeks! Not exactly established, is it?

ONE: But he says he loves me.

TWO: Oh please! He hardly knows you.

ONE: I've seen him virtually every day.

TWO: So what do you know about him?

ONE: Well, he's a painter, he's 22, he holidays in Ibiza, supports Chelsea and he's into Fatboy Slim.

TWO: Very interesting, but what's he like?

ONE: Erm . . . well, he's nice . . . (*Pause*) . . . I suppose he has got a bit of a reputation.

TWO: Oh yeah?

ONE: But he's told me it's totally different with me.

TWO: Look, I don't wanna lecture you, but I know what

I'd do and that's apply the brakes big time. If he really loves you . . . well, he won't mind waiting, will he?

ONE: Maybe.

TWO: Definitely. I just don't want you to do something you'll regret. (*ALL face front*)

ONE: Of course it all sounded so sensible, but as we all know every coin has two sides. (*ONE and THREE turn to face each other, TWO freezes*)

THREE: So how's it going with old Davey boy?

ONE: Pretty well, we've been going steady for two weeks.

THREE: Two weeks! Blimey, you're a pair of old timers!

ONE: Do you think?

THREE: 'Course.

ONE: Dave was suggesting we . . . well, you know, move things on a step or two.

THREE: Oh yeah? Randy wotsit.

ONE: What do you think I should do?

THREE: What do I think you should do? Go for it, you dozy mare. You only live once.

ONE: But do you think it's a bit too soon?

THREE: (*Mimics ONE*) Is it a bit too soon? NO! Who put that thought into your head?

ONE: No one in particular.

THREE: You've been talking to that prudish friend of yours, haven't you?

ONE: No . . . Maybe.

THREE: How many times have I told you to ignore her? She could killjoy for England that girl.

ONE: Oh don't be nasty.

THREE: Listen to me, girl. Dave is well lush and if you don't get in there while you've got the chance, some other bit's gonna step in. I'd be in there myself if I didn't have two kids to look after on my own. Just go for it. Am I right or am I right?

ONE: Maybe.

THREE: Definitely. I don't want you to miss out on something you'll regret. (*ALL face front*)

ONE: So there's the dilemma.

TWO: Two sides of the story.

THREE: Opposite sides of a coin.

ONE: So who did I listen to, I hear you ask.

TWO: Well . . . .

THREE: Come on, spill the beans.

ONE: No, I'm not saying. I hate those neat little conclusions, and I don't want people judging me one way or the other. All I'll say is that Dave and me are together no more.

TWO: That means she didn't.

THREE: Stroll on, it means she did.

ONE: It means, I'll let you draw your own conclusions. Who would you listen to? Who's wise? Who's foolish? And the moral of this tale? Well, I'll let you decide. (*ONE looks at TWO and THREE then back to audience. Blackout*)

TEACHING POINT

When seeking advice from a friend, look for a wise and unbiased counsellor.

BIBLE REFERENCE

Proverbs 14:7

Prayer Diary

The words of a gossip are like choice morsels; they go down to a man's inmost parts.

INTRODUCTION

Here's another sketch about our human desire to gossip, also introducing the theme of confidentiality. I have set the piece after a prayer meeting which the two characters have used as a source for the latest hot gossip. I'm not knocking church prayer meetings. However, I do believe that in the church we must be sensitive about what we 'share' with one another about people's lives and what should remain confidential. For comic effect, the characters in this sketch are vicious gossips with few redeeming qualities. In the church there are often well-meaning individuals who in their desire to 'share' furnish too much information. For example, if a Christian couple are having serious relationship difficulties, is it necessary for the whole church to know all the intimate details to pray effectively?

Here I have used the characters Mabel and Joan from a piece in my last book, called 'Ginger Snaps and Fondant Fancies'. Reference is also made to Father Humphrey, Mary Marshall and Harold the gannet, though none of these appear. The sketch can easily be played by men or women.

Characters: MABEL, JOAN.

Lights come up on MABEL and JOAN who are seated and sipping cups of coffee.

MABEL: Ooh, not a bad turn out tonight, was it Joany, considering.

JOAN: Not bad at all, Mabel love, not bad at all.

MABEL: It's disgusting really though, I mean where is people's commitment?

JOAN: Ooh I know, I couldn't agree more, Mabel.

MABEL: Think about it, Joany. It's the midweek prayer meeting.

JOAN: I know.

MABEL: In my opinion it's the boiler house of the church.

JOAN: Exactly.

MABEL: I mean, without prayer, where would the church be?

JOAN: You're so right, Mabel love, you're so right.

MABEL: One hour! That's all it is, one measly hour.

JOAN: Well it's nothing, is it, in the grand scheme of things.

MABEL: But oh no, people can't tear themselves away from the flipping telly, not even for one hour.

JOAN: Mind you, it's understandable though.

MABEL: What do you mean?

JOAN: Well *Coronation Street*'s hotting up a bit at the moment, isn't it.

MABEL: Ooh you're not wrong there, Joany. Still, in this day and age people can video it, can't they.

JOAN: They just don't think to, do they.

MABEL: No. My Henry said he'd tape it for me tonight – that's if the hopeless lummox can stay awake.

JOAN: Ooh, my Charlie's just the same; drops off every five minutes.

MABEL: Well, it's their age, isn't it. If you ask me, all they do past 65 is eat, sleep and go to the toilet.

JOAN: Mmm.

MABEL: Sad really, my Henry used to be so energetic.

JOAN: My Charlie too. Here, talking about energetic, Father Humphrey looks a bit tired tonight, doesn't he?

MABEL: Ooh I thought that, very jaded. (*Sickly smile to Father Humphrey*) Evening, Father Humphrey, lovely prayer meeting this evening. (*Smile fades*) Ooh, did you see the bags under his eyes?

JOAN: Yeah, it's a real shame, isn't it.

MABEL: Listen, don't tell another soul this, Joany – it's strictly between you and me – but I was chatting to Jill who works at the doctor's surgery outside the Co-op this morning.

JOAN: Oh yes.

MABEL: Apparently he's having terrible trouble with his tummy at the moment; his digestive system's gone all wonky. She absolutely swore me to secrecy, but I thought I'd tell you, just so you can pop it into your prayer diary, you understand.

JOAN: Ooh, I will.

MABEL: You know I don't gossip – that's not my style – but we do need to pray intelligently, don't we.

JOAN: Absolutely Mabel, absolutely.

MABEL: (*Pause*) Ooh, have you seen Mary Marshall over there? She makes you sick.

JOAN: Where?

MABEL: There! Flirting around Father Humphrey like a love-struck teenager.

JOAN: Oh it's disgusting; she should know better at her age.

MABEL: Over him like a rash she is, and look at the amount of make-up she's got caked on. Who does she think she is – Dolly Parton?

JOAN: Well, it's mutton dressed as lamb, isn't it.

MABEL: Having her drool all over him won't do his tummy condition any favours either, will it.

JOAN: No, you're right there, Mabel.

MABEL: That's the only reason she comes to the prayer

meeting you know, for a bit of a flirt. I was watching her during the intercessions, just out of one eye like, and she was in a complete daze, totally unaware of what was being prayed.

JOAN: Was she really?

MABEL: Mmm. Did you know she's directly in front of me on the telephone gossip chain? I mean prayer chain.

JOAN: Is she?

MABEL: Yeah, but do you know. I never know whether to believe a word she says.

JOAN: Oh that's terrible.

MABEL: Tell me about it. She's the worst exaggerator in the whole wide world. You'll never guess what she phoned through to me the other week.

JOAN: Go on.

MABEL: Well, you know old William?

JOAN: Old William? Which one's that?

MABEL: Oh you know, the one with the wonky eye and gammy foot that hands out the hymn books of a Sunday morning.

JOAN: Oh, that William.

MABEL: Yes! Well, anyway, she phones me up, all panicky like, and tells me he's been rushed into hospital with gastroenteritis and an inflamed intestine.

JOAN: Ooh, that sounds nasty.

MABEL: Ah, you wait. It turns out he had a mild case of trapped wind.

JOAN: No!

MABEL: Yeah, would you believe it? I mean, how can I pray intelligently with her spinning ridiculous yarns like that?

JOAN: Mind you, I wish my Charlie would get a dose of that.

MABEL: What, trapped wind?

JOAN: Yeah, he's got a severe case of the opposite problem, if you get my drift.

MABEL: Oh Joany, no!

JOAN: 'Better out than in,' he says. Oh, it's absolutely revolting.

MABEL: We're absolute martyrs, aren't we, Joany love. I mean, what we have to put up with, with those two.

JOAN: (*Pause*) I see your mate Harold's in this evening.

MABEL: What, old Harold the gannet? 'Course he is. You know Harold – if there's food, he's there.

JOAN: He polished off all the chocolate Hob Nobs in under five minutes.

MABEL: You know, if there wasn't coffee and biscuits after the prayer meeting, you can bet your bottom dollar he wouldn't come. I'm sorry if I sound all judgemental, 'cos you know that's not my style, but he really is the limit.

JOAN: I notice that Jonathan, the nice young youth leader, isn't here tonight.

MABEL: Mmm, I noticed that, and Father Humphrey prayed a very odd prayer for him, didn't he.

JOAN: Funny you should say that, 'cos I thought he was very cagey about him. I wonder what all that's about.

MABEL: Maybe I should have a quiet little word with Father H, now Mary's prized herself away from him.

JOAN: I think that's an excellent idea, Mabel.

MABEL: Really?

JOAN: It would come best from you.

MABEL: Nothing heavy handed, just a gentle little dig for information.

JOAN: Well, you're well known for your sensitivity, aren't you.

MABEL: Because of course I've got no interest personally in what the problem is.

JOAN: Well, it's not your concern, is it.

MABEL: But it's handy to know these things, just so I can put them in my prayer diary, you understand.

JOAN: Precisely.

MABEL: And I find it so much more effective if I can pray intelligently.

JOAN: My sentiments exactly.

MABEL: (*Pause*) Yes, I think I'll have a word with him now.

JOAN: Well, it's the courteous and Christian thing to do, isn't it?

MABEL: 'Course it is. Right, you go and get us a coffee refill, Joany love, and I'll have a quiet word. Rendezvous back here in five.

JOAN: Okay. Good luck. (*JOAN exits*)

MABEL: (*Deep breaths, straightens her collar and catches Father Humphrey's attention*) Father Humphrey . . . Father Humphrey, ah, just a quiet word with you if I may. (*She exits, walking towards Father Humphrey as the lights fade to blackout*)

TEACHING POINT

There is a time for everything; a time to share and a time for confidentiality.

BIBLE REFERENCE

Proverbs 26:22

Smelly Kenny

Rescue those being led away to death; hold back those staggering towards slaughter.

INTRODUCTION

Although there are a few laughs at various points in this sketch, overall it is designed to pack a hard punch to its audience. Using the age-old problem of bullying and its terrible long-term effects, the piece highlights the teaching in Proverbs about just standing by when the helpless suffer.

Rob has no redeeming qualities, either as a child or 20 years later. Simon was easily coerced into bullying with Rob, but having seen its tragic consequences is now repentant. Apart from a few cries for help, Kenny is a non-speaking part: he remains 'faceless', with his back to the audience. The piece can stand alone or will work well with teaching about helping the oppressed and repentance.

Characters: ROB, SIMON, KENNY.

KENNY is sitting centre stage with his back to the audience. ROB and SIMON enter and deliver their first lines – they are unaware of KENNY at present.

ROB: Hold yer horses, Si. I don't understand what the point of this is. (*They stop and pause*) Why have you brought us here? Simon?

SIMON: Brings back memories, don't it.

ROB: Yeah, I suppose. Now, let's go.

SIMON: Nearly 20 years, but it all still comes flooding back.

ROB: That's what memories tend to do; now come on. (*He tries unsuccessfully to lead SIMON away*)

SIMON: (*In a world of his own*) I had my first kiss over there.

ROB: Where?

SIMON: Behind the bike shed, believe it or not. Sounds like a bit of a cliché, doesn't it. But it's totally true . . . Amy Saunders.

ROB: (*Shocked*) You got a snog out of Amy Saunders?!

SIMON: No, not a snog. We were only seven at the time.

ROB: Oh.

SIMON: Just a little peck, but I tell you it felt good. I can remember it like it was yesterday. It all started when her best friend Clare Bridges uttered those immortal words. . . .

ROB: (*Becomes Clare Bridges*) 'Scuse me, but my mate fancies you.

SIMON: (*Becomes his younger self*) Eh?

ROB: My mate Amy Saunders fancies you.

SIMON: So what?

ROB: She wants to kiss you.

SIMON: UGGHHH!! She's a ...girl!

ROB: Well of course she's a girl.

SIMON: Yuk! I don't wanna kiss a girl.

ROB: Why?

SIMON: 'Cos they . . . they . . . they all smell.

ROB: Ugh, that means you like kissing boys.

SIMON: No I don't!

ROB: Yes you do.

SIMON: Don't.

ROB: Do.

SIMON: DON'T!

ROB: DO!!

SIMON: DON'T!!

ROB: (*Pause*) Prove it then.

SIMON: How?

ROB: Kiss Amy Saunders. (*SIMON and ROB revert to their original characters*) So, you kissed Amy Saunders?

SIMON: Yep, to prove my seven-year-old masculinity I tasted Amy Saunders' ruby-red lips under the watchful eye of Clare Bridges behind that very same bike shed – over 20 years ago.

ROB: And as future years proved, you were the first of many, very many! Look, are you ready to go now?

SIMON: That must have been about the same time you started your reign of terror.

ROB: Oh Simon, don't do this.

SIMON: Only in a small way to start with, maybe. You had me as your accomplice – not that I blame *you*. No, I can't pass the buck on to anyone else for my actions.

ROB: If it helps you, Simon, give me the blame. I take full responsibility for what. . . .

SIMON: (*Interrupts*) NO!! No, I could of stopped you but I didn't. I just stood by and watched . . . and then joined in. Well, why not? He was an easy target, wasn't he? Kenny Regis.

ROB: We were just kids, Simon. Kids are cruel. It's a sad fact of life: we were just kids. (*ROB and SIMON become their seven-year-old selves*) Stinky, smelly Kenny. Stinky, smelly Kenny. Everybody hates him 'cos he's a big fat benny! (*ROB starts to poke KENNY who is now visible*)

SIMON: (*Joins in prodding and insulting KENNY*) Yeah, you're a big fat benny, Kenny.

ROB: Your mum's a fat old bag, and she smells too.

SIMON: Yeah, your whole family all smell like poo!

ROB: And you all wet your beds too, and that's why the whole school hates you.

SIMON: You smell of wee and poo and everybody hates you.

ROB: Even the teachers hate you. I heard Miss Wilton yesterday say, 'Ooh, I hate that Kenny Regis 'cos he's a big smelly benny!'

SIMON: Yeah, and she said you'll never have any friends or ever get married or ever have children and everyone will always hate you. (*Both laugh at KENNY and push and slap him*)

ROB: Now give us your lunch money, Kenny. Benny Kenny, smelly benny Kenny. (*They both continue insulting KENNY as they physically search his pockets for money*)

KENNY: (*High-pitched squeal*) Stop, stop. STOP!! (*Short pause, ROB and SIMON revert to original characters*)

ROB: (*Pause*) We were just kids, Simon.

SIMON: Can't you just admit you were wrong, Rob, even now?

ROB: What do you want me to say?

SIMON: Eight years it continued, didn't it? Eight years. Were we still 'just kids' at 15? Remember the school disco? The school disco where I re-acquainted myself with Amy Saunders. (*Background eighties music can be heard. SIMON becomes his 15-year-old self, ROB becomes a 15-year-old Amy Saunders. They are slow dancing*)

ROB: (*As Amy Saunders*) Ooh, I love that Simon le Bon out of Duran Duran. Do you, Si?

SIMON: Yeah, he's all right I suppose.

ROB: And that George Michael out of Wham. He can wake me up before he go-goes, anytime.

SIMON: Have you finished, Amy? You're upsetting my male
         sensibilities.

ROB: Ahhhh! I'm all yours tonight, hunny bunny. . . .
        'Ere, watch your hands, mate – I ain't that easy!

SIMON: Oh come on, Ames, loosen up a bit. You know I
         love you.

ROB: Oh yeah, Si; I'm sure you know all about love at 15.

SIMON: Yeah, but I'm well mature for my age – everyone
         says so.

ROB: Oh look over there. (*ROB indicates KENNY who is
        still in opening position, centre stage with back to
        the audience*)

SIMON: Eh?

ROB: Look. Kenny Regis sitting on his own in the corner.
        I feel a bit sorry for him – I don't think he's got any
        friends.

SIMON: That's no surprise: he's a right saddo. KENNY NO
         MATES, KENNY NO MATES . . . (*As SIMON
         begins to chant, ROB reverts to his 15-year-old self
         and joins in*) . . . KENNY NO MATES, KENNY
         NO MATES!!

SIMON: (*Reverts to adult for just one line*) And that same
         evening under the influence of the vodka we
         sneaked into the disco disguised as cream soda, we
         finished him off, really finished him off. (*SIMON
         reverts to 15-year-old self*)

ROB: Ah look who it is, Si. Kenny. Our best mate Kenny.
        Ooh I wonder if I can squeeze past all his hundreds
        of friends. (*ROB and SIMON are obviously drunk.
        They laugh and pretend to squeeze through an imag-
        inary crowd*) Enjoy the party did you, Kenny?

SIMON: Did you get a snog, Kenny?

ROB: Smelly Kenny.

SIMON: Smelly Kenny the benny. (*They are in hysterics*)

ROB: Want some vodka, oops, I mean cream soda?

SIMON: Well answer him then, you freak. (*KENNY shakes his head*)

ROB: (*Viciously throws vodka into KENNY'S face*) You're pathetic.

SIMON: A waste of space.

ROB: I don't know how I've put up with you all these years. Your miserable, ugly little face.

SIMON: Oh, I think he's wet himself, Rob.

ROB: Uggh! It's disgusting. Well, we've always known he's a bed wetter.

SIMON: Yeah, smelly Kenny benny the bed wetter.

ROB: Maybe we should put him out of his misery. No friends, no birds, no life, no future. It would be kindest really. (*He smacks KENNY'S face, then SIMON copies him*) It might be best if you didn't see this.

(*ROB takes his bottle out of its bag, and puts it over KENNY'S head. KENNY struggles but Simon restrains him. Then follows a short, sharp violent choreographed one-way fight, in which ROB and SIMON pummel KENNY. After a series of head and body blows KENNY falls to the floor utterly dejected. KENNY should always remain with his back to the audience. There is a silent pause as ROB and SIMON look down at the sobbing KENNY. ROB and SIMON revert to their original adult characters*)

ROB: (*Pause*) We were just kids, Si.

SIMON: Do you know he never did have any real friends, never had a girlfriend, never moved away from home. A tragic loner.

ROB: Yeah, well some people are like that – it's life.

SIMON: But we made him like that. Don't you see?

ROB: No, I don't. Now are you coming or not?

SIMON: Sorry.

ROB: What?

SIMON: Sorry. That's what his suicide note read. Just sorry.

ROB: What was that then? A message to his mumsy or a description of his life?

SIMON: (*Looks at ROB in disgust*) You just don't care, do you?

ROB: No, I don't. I never did like him. Why should I pretend to now?

SIMON: Why did you come to the funeral?

ROB: I dunno. Seemed like the right thing to do. Anyway, it'll be good to have a few jars with the old school gang. Now are you coming? Oh, I'll see you in the pub. (*ROB exits*)

SIMON: (*Pause*) I don't know if you can hear me, Kenny. (*KENNY gets up and takes his opening position*) I had the power to make everything different, but I was a stupid little coward. I stood by and let it all happen. I joined in – I admit that. For what it's worth, I'm sorry. I'm really sorry. (*SIMON slowly exits as lights fade to blackout*)

TEACHING POINT

When you see someone suffering at the hands of another, don't turn your back and claim ignorance – step in and help them.

BIBLE REFERENCE

Proverbs 24:11–12

So, Who'll Take the Blame?

He who conceals his sins does not prosper, but whoever confesses and renounces them finds mercy.

INTRODUCTION

The sketch is an ensemble piece and requires four actors who skip between a variety of parts. Its subject is that of blame: do we accept it when necessary or always pass the buck? It looks at some typical human responses and compares them to those of Christ, who not only willingly accepted blame but took it a step further by accepting it when he was totally innocent.

This sketch will work best as a short, punchy piece, using quick choreographed movements and if possible a variety of character voices. Comical at the beginning, it finishes with a challenging image of the cross. The ensemble should work on making this ending powerful, yet cringe free.

Characters: ONE, TWO, THREE, FOUR.

Lights come up on the four actors. We hear the musical theme of the News.

ONE: Today's tragic disaster is likely to have left dozens killed and many more injured. As the family and friends of the victims begin to come to terms with the reality of today's events, we ask the question on everyone's lips: Who is to blame?

TWO: Not me, I'm afraid.

THREE: Well, it's certainly not me.

FOUR: Don't look at me.

ONE: Minister, may I put it to you that this is further evidence that increased investment is required in this area to make. . . .

TWO: If I may just interject here, of course this is a terrible tragedy and my deepest sympathy is with the families of all the victims, but let's just take a look at our record since being in government, and put this whole thing into perspective. A 17.1 per cent increase in cumulative spending over the same period last year, which in real terms represents a 29.7 per cent gross investment inflation per capita, compared to a 12.7 per cent decrease in negative influx spending by the previous government.

ONE: Well, thank you Minister. As ever you've made things perfectly clear, but the question of the people remains: Who is to blame?

TWO: Well, erm. . . .

ONE: Come now, Minister. A disaster of this magnitude deserves solid answers and swift action.

TWO: Well, if I were pushed into apportioning blame to a specific area, I would have to say it was society as a whole.

ONE, THREE, and FOUR stand and become rowdy politicians in a House of Commons style debate.

ONE: Order! Order!

TWO: Madam Speaker, this storm of abuse is intolerable when I'm trying to answer the dishonourable gentleman's accusations.

THREE: How can you defend your government's broken promises in relation to the National Health Service?

TWO: Ah well, that's the economic climate.

FOUR: What else is there to blame for the steady increase in unemployment figures, except for sheer ministerial incompetence?

TWO: Hmm, now that's due to the totally unpredictable strength of the Deutschmark.

ONE: And how and why in the light of yet another fatal disaster, can the Minister stick to his crumbling policies on public transport and safety?

TWO: Well, my mother-in-law told me to!

ONE: I'm sorry, Minister, that's simply not good enough. You can't dump the blame for everything elsewhere. You must take some responsibility.

TWO: (*Stuttering*) Well maybe some of the blame has to fall on. . . .

ONE: Who?

TWO: (*Pause*) The Chief Executive of Fat Cat Incorporated.

ONE, TWO and FOUR become group of reporters. THREE is a chief executive trying to make a statement.

ONE/TWO/FOUR: (*Pushing and shoving*) Mr Fat Cat?

THREE: (*Stands on chair, surrounded*) Ladies and gentlemen, I have a brief statement to make on behalf of Fat Cat Incorporated. If you bear with me I'll read it in full. (*Unfolds statement, puts glasses on and reads*) It's not our fault. Thank you, ladies and gentlemen. At this stage I have no further comment to make. (*Scene of disruption*)

ONE: Come off it, Mr Fat Cat! It's not our fault? That's a bit lame, isn't it?

THREE: I repeat, at this stage I have no further comment to make.

TWO: The victims' families and the public at large have a right to know who is to blame.

THREE: Well, how about computer error? Will that do?

ONE: No, not good enough.

THREE: Erm, well it's a tricky one.

ONE: Come on, we're waiting.

THREE: Well. . . . (*As THREE stutters, ONE and TWO stamp and chant WHO, WHO, WHO . . .*)

FOUR: I'll take the blame.

ONE: What?!

TWO: What did he say?!

THREE: What?!

FOUR: I'll take the blame.

FOUR is pushed into a chair by ONE, TWO and THREE who are standing behind him in a semicircle looking threatening.

ONE: So why would you do that then?

TWO: Who are you?

THREE: Go on, answer then.

ONE: He's lost his tongue.

TWO: Too ashamed to speak.

THREE: Come on, mate. Speak up. (*Pause . . . ONE, TWO and THREE move in closer*)

ONE: He's bonkers.

TWO: If you don't speak, we can't defend you.

THREE: Let's hear your side of the story.

ONE: Think up a defence.

TWO: Make up some excuses.

THREE: Get the court of public opinion on your side. (*Pause*)

ONE: Do you realise that silence is seen as a sign of guilt?

TWO: You'll get blamed for the lot.

THREE: The disaster.

ONE: The suffering.

TWO: The death and destruction.

ONE: Oh, please yourself then. But I'll tell you ... they're gonna crucify you.

TWO and THREE roughly grab an arm of FOUR and yank him up to the crucifixion position. FREEZE.

ONE: Who'll take the blame?

TWO: Who'll take the blame?

THREE: Who'll take the blame?

FOUR: I'll take the blame.

Freeze and hold as music is brought up and lights fade to blackout.

TEACHING POINT

To confess our mistakes and accept blame is to show great courage and dignity.

BIBLE REFERENCE

Proverbs 28:13

Ten Thousand Empty Wineskins

A man's wisdom gives him patience.

INTRODUCTION

The Bible often teaches us the importance of patience, even citing it as part of the fruit of the Spirit. In this proverb it is linked with wisdom; so what is the wisdom of patience? I'm sure there are many possible answers to this question, but in this sketch I have concentrated on the link between patiently waiting and procrastination. There are times when waiting patiently for God's direction is obviously the proper thing to do. However, it can be easy to procrastinate while waiting.

The setting here is the period between Christ's ascension and Pentecost. I have used a copious amount of dramatic licence to imagine a conversation between three of the disciples. The Bible doesn't tell us much about the time between these two events, though we can assume the disciples were buoyant as they returned to Jerusalem to pray and wait for the Holy Spirit. This is a good example of patience without procrastination. But imagine a new scenario of the disciples waiting and doing nothing! A sense of boredom and dissatisfaction would arise, possibly leading to frustration and squabbles. Please note that I do not suggest anything like this actually happened – I merely use this as an illustration to make a point. The success of the sketch rests on effective comic performances and building a sense of boredom and frustration between the characters.

Characters: PETER, JAMES, JOHN.

Lights come up. JAMES is flicking playing cards into a hat, which is irritating PETER. JOHN is having forty winks.

PETER: (*Irritated*) Will you pack that in!

JAMES: What?

PETER: THAT!

JAMES: Why? It's not harming you.

PETER: Yes it is; it's getting on my nerves. How anyone can flick cards into a hat for six hours non-stop – well, it's totally beyond me.

JAMES: Why don't you have a go? It might calm you down.

PETER: No thank you. And for your information I don't need calming down.

JAMES: Whatever you say.

PETER: Well I do say.

Pause. PETER irritates JOHN, trying to wake him up by tickling his ear with grass, blowing on him, etc.

PETER: John . . . John . . . Wakey, wakey.

JOHN: Get off, will you!

JAMES: Leave him alone, Peter.

PETER: Ooh, what's this then? Sticking up for your brother?

JAMES: What if it is?

PETER: (*Mimics JAMES*) 'Ooh, leave him alone, Peter.'

JAMES: Sometimes you can be so pathetic.

PETER: Oh, pathetic am I?

JOHN: Boys, boys, boys! It's very flattering having you argue over me but, if it's all the same to you, I'd prefer it if you didn't.

PETER: Well, Hallelujah! He's in the land of the living at last. Had a nice kip, have you?

JOHN: Yeah, lovely thanks.

PETER: You completely amaze me: you sleep more than a sloth!

JOHN: Well, it passes the time, don't it? Chuck us over the Pringles, James.

JAMES: (*Tips empty tube upside down*) Sorry bruv, all gone.

PETER: What!

JAMES: All gone! Well, you know what it's like. Once you pop you can't. . . .

PETER: (*Interrupts*) Yes we know! (*Sulking*) I only had about two of them, and sleeping beauty here didn't get a look in at all. You're so selfish, sitting there on your own scoffing the lot.

JAMES: Well I'm sorry.

PETER: What about the Roses?

JAMES: Eh?

PETER: The Roses! I suppose you've woofed all of them down too.

JAMES: There's a few coffee creams left.

PETER: UGGHHH!! Trust you to leave the most revolting ones. Well I hope you're sick.

JAMES: Thank you, Peter. That's very kind of you.

JOHN: Will you two pipe down – you're wearing me out!

PETER: Well he started it.

JAMES: I did not.

PETER: Yes you did, flicking them stupid cards.

JAMES: Huh, it was you with your constant moaning.

PETER: Well I wouldn't have to moan if you weren't such an infuriating and greedy slob.

JOHN: THAT'S ENOUGH! Let's all just cool down a bit: deep breaths. . . . That's better. Now, why don't we all play a nice game?

PETER: Like what?

JOHN: Well how about . . . I know, 'I Spy with my Little Eye'.

PETER/JAMES: (*Together*) OH NO!

JOHN: What?

PETER: We're outside in the middle of nowhere, John. We exhausted all possibilities two days ago. Sky, sun, trees, grass, sheep plop!

JOHN: Well, you think of something then.

JAMES: (*Pause. Sings quietly to tune of 'Ten Green Bottles'*) Ten thousand empty wineskins hanging on a wall . . . (*PETER and JOHN stare*) Okay, okay, it was just a suggestion.

PETER: Oh this is ridiculous! Three days we've been waiting here – three days! We must look like a bunch of right prize prunes.

JOHN: You just need to be patient, Peter.

PETER: (*Impatiently*) Patient! I am the epitome of patience. My friends all call me Patient Pete. Don't talk to me about patience.

JAMES: (*Slightly sarcastic*) Whatever you say, Patient Pete.

PETER: What's that supposed to mean? If you've got something to say, just say it.

JAMES: Well come on; be honest Peter. You are just a little bit impulsive sometimes, aren't you?

PETER: Me, impulsive? Give me one good example.

JOHN: Well, how about the time just before Jesus' arrest, when you hacked that bloke's ear off?

PETER: Oh you always bring that up.

JOHN: Well, it's not very easy to forget, is it?

PETER: Look, I was defending our Lord. What can I say? There are casualties of war.

JAMES: Jesus didn't agree with that though, did he? He was rather more interested in sticking the guy's ear back on.

PETER: Yes all right, maybe that wasn't my wisest move ever, but you two can't talk.

JAMES: Why?

JOHN: Yeah, why?

PETER: Remember your little request to our Lord?

JAMES: Oh here he goes again.

PETER: 'Father, if it is possible can we sit at your right hand at the throne of grace?' How childish can you get?

JOHN: Well, he didn't say no, did he?

PETER: Didn't say yes either.

JAMES: Oh give it a rest, will you? We're supposed to be the inner group of Jesus' closest disciples. Look at us: we're behaving like a bunch of kids.

PETER: Well, where is he? He said he was coming back soon.

JOHN: He didn't say that exactly.

PETER: That bloke in the white did. What was it he said? Something like 'Jesus will come back in the same way he went into heaven,' or words to that effect.

JOHN: But he didn't say when – could be a fortnight, could be a month!

PETER: Oh don't be so daft! He wouldn't have us hanging round like lemons for a month, would he?

JOHN: Well, maybe he has come back and we've missed him.

PETER: Missed him! He's coming back in a blaze of glory. I don't think anyone will be missing him.

JAMES: Quieten down, Peter. I think what we've been missing here is the point.

PETER: Do expand, oh wise one.

JAMES: Well, we know Jesus is coming back but we don't know when, right?

PETER: Right.

JAMES: We also know at some point he's sending us a helper.

PETER: Yes, and boy do we need it.

JAMES: So why are we just sitting around here waiting for something to happen?

PETER: Patience, my dear boy, patience.

JAMES: There's nothing wrong with patience, Peter – patience is good. But procrastination is bad.

JOHN: Well said, bruv.

JAMES: While we're waiting, what's to stop us doing something?

PETER: Like what?

JAMES: Get together with the other disciples – we need to sort out a replacement for Judas for starters. Pray together; plan how we're going to fulfil the great commission. Get ourselves ready.

JOHN: Well I'm up for it, James. What about you, Peter?

PETER: Yes, well, it's a good point I suppose . . . I don't know though; maybe we should wait a bit longer.

JAMES: Well I'm going to find the others, with or without you. Are you coming, John?

JOHN: Yeah, definitely. Come on, Peter, it'll be great.

PETER: (*Pause*) I'm not sure.

JAMES: Come on, John, we've wasted enough time already. (*JAMES strides off, JOHN looks towards PETER then follows*)

PETER: (*Pause. He has a go at flicking the cards etc., then starts singing*) Ten thousand empty wineskins hanging on a wall. . . . Hang on a minute, boys. James, John, wait for me. (*PETER rushes off, lights fade to blackout*)

TEACHING POINT

Patience is wise; procrastination is not.

BIBLE REFERENCE

Proverbs 19:11

Trust Me, I'm an Estate Agent

The LORD abhors dishonest scales, but accurate weights are his delight.

INTRODUCTION

With apologies to the many reputable estate agents out there. This sketch was conceived at a time when my sister was having a nightmare selling her flat, and an estate agent became the person I chose to illustrate dishonest scales. Often we try to cover up any falsehood by describing it not as lying, but as being 'conservative with the truth' or some such thing. Proverbs 11:1 uses strong language when it says that the Lord abhors dishonesty, and this piece illustrates this point.

The strongest actor should play Eddie, who is sly and comical. You will need few props to perform the sketch, but to make the piece look tight it is important that the cast identify the space where each of the rooms is.

Characters: EDDIE, GEOFF, MR CREDULOUS, MRS CREDULOUS.

Lights come up on EDDIE and GEOFF looking around the house.

EDDIE:	Oh dear, oh dear, oh dear. What a right two and eight this place is in!
GEOFF:	Not exactly luxury accommodation, is it?
EDDIE:	Understatement of the year that, Geoff, understatement of the year! I mean, look at it!
GEOFF:	Yeah, but as a little one-bedroom flat for a first-

138

time buyer it has got some quite nice little touches though, Eddie.

EDDIE: (*Shocked*) Like what?

GEOFF: Well. . . . Well, now you come to mention it, I can't think of any.

EDDIE: Of course you can't, Geoff – the whole thing looks like something out of Beirut. Take this lounge for a start.

GEOFF: Hard to find any tempting selling points, I grant you.

EDDIE: Creaky floorboards, flaky ceiling, and walls that aren't so much damp as sopping.

GEOFF: But you love a challenge, Eddie. That's why you're our number one salesman. I bet you've sussed an angle already.

EDDIE: Well, maybe I have, Geoffrey, maybe I have. (*EDDIE claps hands together, GEOFF freezes and MR and MRS CREDULOUS enter*) Ah, Mr and Mrs Credulous, welcome both of you to one of the hottest properties currently on our books. If I've had one enquiry about this place, I've had a dozen. Yes, well, here is the lounge, and quite a lounge it is too, I think you'll agree. (*MR and MRS CREDULOUS have looks of stunned silence*) . . . Hello, hello! Quite something, isn't it?

MR CRED: Yes well, it's not quite what we were expecting, is it dear?

MRS CRED: No.

EDDIE: What, a little bit too luxurious for you?

MR CRED: No, it's just. . . . Well, look at the state of the floor and ceilings.

EDDIE: Mmm, very art nouveau, isn't it? Incredibly in

nowadays.

MR CRED: But the walls are rather, how can I put it? A bit on the damp side.

EDDIE: Oh no no no no no! I think you're rather missing the point of the ambience of this particular room. I can see if you look at it at face value you would think damp, but that is a specially created design. Yes, it's what we nowadays call the 'distressed look'. It's the current trend in interior decoration. Do you watch *Changing Rooms*?

MRS CRED: Ooh yes; it's one of my favourites.

EDDIE: Well, this particular deeply distressed look is advocated by the chap on that show – what's his name? The one who always wears purple crushed velvet.

MRS CRED: Lawrence.

EDDIE: That's him! According to him, apparently this look is set to become the next big thing. Come to think of it, I believe Tom Cruise and Nicole Kidman have got it in their dining room.

MRS CRED: Really?

EDDIE: Yes. Why don't you both just step back and imagine how you could impress all your friends? (*EDDIE claps, MR and MRS CREDU-LOUS freeze, GEOFF breaks his freeze and rejoins the action*)

GEOFF: (*Crouching*) Blimey, if you thought the lounge was bad, look at the state of the bathroom!

EDDIE: (*Joins him, bends over*) Jeepers creepers! I've never seen one so small that you can't stand up to . . . well, you know!

GEOFF: Not small, Eddie! Compact if you don't mind.

Remember it's compact.

EDDIE: Sorry, Geoff, a slip of the tongue. Compact it is. Manageable and compact. (*EDDIE claps, GEOFF freezes and MR and MRS CRED break freeze*) So what do you think?

MR CRED: It's a little bit. . . . What's the word I'm looking for?

MRS CRED: Small?

MR CRED: Yes, a little bit on the small side.

EDDIE: Compact, Mr Credulous. Economic, manageable and compact.

MR CRED: But I can't even stand up straight.

EDDIE: Well, I think that's rather sexist of you.

MR CRED: What?

EDDIE: Well, think about it. Mrs Credulous doesn't actually need to stand up, does she? Do you Mrs Credulous?

MRS CRED: Well, no. I suppose you've got a point.

EDDIE: Of course I do.

MR CRED: That's as maybe but you couldn't swing a dead cat around in here.

EDDIE: Let's just examine that statement shall we, Mr Credulous? How many times in your life have you ever had the need or indeed desire to swing around a dead cat?

MR CRED: Well, never.

EDDIE: There you are. And if you did I'm sure you'd have the RSPCA down on you like a ton of bricks. (*EDDIE claps, MR and MRS CREDULOUS freeze, GEOFF breaks freeze*)

GEOFF: (*Looks up*) That is totally unbelievable.

EDDIE: Oh now what?

GEOFF: Here, in the bedroom.

EDDIE: (*Joins GEOFF*) Oh my life! Look at the size of it.

GEOFF: I've seen some holes in ceilings in my life, but this one just about takes the biscuit.

EDDIE: This is a complete nightmare, or a practical joke. I bet Jeremy Beadle's gonna come charging through that door any second now.

GEOFF: Come on Eddie, just think of the job satisfaction when you manage to bamboozle some poor blighters into buying this complete dump.

EDDIE: Yeah, I suppose you're right. It'll be my crowning moment, my *coup de grâce*. (*EDDIE claps, GEOFF freezes, MR and MRS CREDULOUS break freeze*) And now, the bedroom. (*MR and MRS CREDULOUS look up in silence and shock*) I can see it's rendered you both speechless once again.

MR CRED: Do you take us for a pair of fools?

EDDIE: I'm sorry?

MR CRED: For pity's sake, man, have you not seen that thumping great big hole?

EDDIE: (*Surprised*) Hole! What hole?

MR CRED: THAT ONE! The one the size of the Grand Canyon.

EDDIE: Oh that! That's not a hole. No, that's your air conditioning.

MR CRED: Air conditioning?

MRS CRED: Air conditioning!

EDDIE: Mmm, good isn't it? Absolutely huge over in the States.

MR CRED: (*Defeated*) Are you sure?

EDDIE: Yes, positive. They have a great slogan: 'The wholesome way to natural air conditioning.'

	Quite clever, I thought.
MR CRED:	Mmm, very clever.
MRS CRED:	I just don't know about all this; it's all so different from what I'd expected.
EDDIE:	Well, it's highly modern I grant you, but with a place like this, you'll be streets ahead of the crowd.
MRS CRED:	Do you think so?
MR CRED:	Do you really think so?
EDDIE:	(*Pause*) Of course! Trust me, I'm an estate agent. (*They all freeze, fade to blackout*)

TEACHING POINT

All forms of dishonesty, however we dress them up, displease God.

BIBLE REFERENCE

Proverbs 11:1

An Unforgettable Christmas

A man of many companions may come to ruin, but there is a friend who sticks closer than a brother.

INTRODUCTION

Amid all the tinsel and laughter of the festive season lurks the tragedy of many lives ruled by loneliness and depression. I wrote this piece to expose the other side of a typical happy Christmas. As John's story unfolds, we see a once successful man ruined by unemployment and relationship breakdown – to the point of his considering suicide. The subject matter may seem dark, but the piece has many upbeat moments. It illustrates Proverbs' teaching about the importance of befriending the friendless and lonely. The monologue has a running time of around 20 minutes, so is intended for performance by an experienced actor. It is a good idea to create a detailed set, based on a careful study of the text.

Character: JOHN.

As the lights go up we hear the end of the national anthem. JOHN, who is sitting asleep on his armchair, is holding an empty glass and a Pot Noodle on his lap. The final bars of the anthem wake him up.

JOHN: Oh no! That's three straight years I've done that: miss the Queen's speech. (*He moves in his chair and the Pot Noodle falls. The noodles have solidified in the pot and the fork is stuck. He pours a large drink*)

I never used to miss it. Part of the perfect Christmas. Open the prezzies in the morning, have a slap-up Christmas lunch, watch the Queen's speech, then doze off during *Chitty Chitty Bang Bang*. I know they show her again at tea time but it's not the same, is it. That's like watching the repeat. At 3 o'clock it's live . . . well, obviously it's not actually live, 'cos it's on the radio earlier. In fact it's recorded days, weeks before Christmas. I mean you can buy a copy of the *Sun* on the 21st of December, or whenever, and it's got a transcript of the whole speech, with a little quote saying, 'Another royal exclusive from your fun loving *Sun*!'

(*He plays around with a variety of snacks by the side of his chair, eats a cheese football, grimaces, then spits it out*) UGGGHHH!! Why do we buy cheese footballs at Christmas? They taste like vomit. (*Starts throwing them at bin*) Not bad for target practice though! DATES! I mean, dates. Are they even available in ASDA if it's not December? I think not. It's ridiculous: brandy snaps, Twiglets, those diagonal cheese savouries, craters full of nuts. No wonder Christmas is so flipping expensive. Now nuts, I must admit they are a bit different. (*He goes to table where there is a bowl of nuts*) A lot of hassle but very nice. Monkey nuts are my favourite, mainly 'cos I never quite got the hang of the nut crackers. (*Eats nuts and starts choking. Takes a swig of vodka straight from the bottle to stop it*) That'll do the trick. Now where's the TV guide? (*Hunts through a pile of papers and magazines*) Ah, here we are. Now what classic movies have we got on today? Ah, here we are. (*Starts singing*) 'The hills are alive with the sound of music, ah ah ah agghhhh' (*Song trails off into noise of strangulation*) Every year, it drives you mad. I've never

actually stayed awake for the duration of that one. I'd have
to be pumped with a few shots of adrenalin first. (*Sings
James Bond theme, ding dinga ling ling etc.*) That's more
like it. I mean, what would Christmas and bank holidays be
like without a good old Bond movie? Now, which one is it?
Thunderball – good, a Sean Connery one. That Roger
Moore, eyebrow acting in one easy lesson. (*He attempts
impressions of both Connery and Moore*) Ah, Miss
Moneypenny . . . Mish Munnepenne . . . Aha, 'A spoonful
of sugar makes the medicine do down, in the most . . . in
the most . . . delightful way.' (*He can't remember the word
'delightful' for the first few tries*) Oh, that was on at five
past twelve so I've missed it anyway. So, *Thunderball* it is.
That's on at 5.55. Now, if I can just get through the next
two-and-a-half hours. (*He wanders around picking up and
putting down books and papers and starts looking at
Christmas cards*)

You might think for a sad old loner I've got quite a number
of cards, but I suppose I ought to come clean on this one.
You see, about a week ago I only had four cards. My sister
in Australia, now hers came in early November 'cos she
likes to make sure it's not late. Mum and Dad's. Rob, my
university pal who's currently doing a panto in Morecambe.
And this is the best one – I think you'll be quite impressed:
Tony and Cherie Blair. Surprised? Well, don't get too excited. Apparently the Labour Party have targeted my postal
code prefix for a pre-election push. Still, it's a nice thought.
. . . Creeps!! So there they are, the sacred four. Now I said
to myself if I get one more a day until Christmas Eve that'll
be ten. Now double figures, that's socially acceptable, but
since Jeffrey Archer's got more chance of becoming Prime
Minister than I have of getting ten Christmas cards, I decid-

ed to cheat and get out last year's. Well, the last three years' actually. I keep them in a box in case of an emergency. (*Produces a box*) I mean, if I had a guest on, say, December 23rd, and I only had four cards, they would immediately be put off. However, as it is now, a guest would be highly impressed. 'Goodness me, John,' they would exclaim, 'you must have a very wide circle of friends.' Nobody did visit on the 23rd – but you just don't know. You could get a visitor anytime. (*He closes his eyes. Doorbell rings once . . . twice . . . long single ring*) That doorbell you might have heard, it's not actually my doorbell. It's actually my imagination. Often I hear my bell ring. I imagine answering the door to all manner of interesting people: actors, politicians, vets, computer engineers, library assistants. . . . I invite them in, we talk, laugh, drink (*Pours a large drink . . . bell rings*) 'But how do you know it's not really your bell?' I hear you say. Because my bell is broken and, anyway, I know, because even when it worked it never rang. Never rang.

What was I saying . . . Ah, the cards . . . Yes, so out came last year's, two years' ago and three years' ago. Now three years ago I was still at the office. It was a few months before I had become 'surplus to requirements': 'I'm very sorry, Mr Sharpe, believe me your twelve years' long hard service makes this job even harder than it already is but, what with the economy as it is, the old firm is feeling the pinch and the advertising and marketing department, like the others, has to suffer. I'm sure you understand.' NO! (*Blows raspberry*) Anyway, three Christmases ago some bright spark in the office thought it would be a good idea to send everybody a card. Well, of course the whole thing escalated and it all got out of hand. I was sending cards to people whom I occasionally rubbed shoulders with in the canteen. I was receiving cards from people whose only communication with me in the year had been the odd e-mail. Swimming in cards I was. I started to study the quality of the cards to see who liked me most. Now, the ultimate card is the one bought separately; that shows real effort, true friendship. Other qualities I looked for were cards that were thick enough not to flop over before Christmas. Envelopes that you can't see through. In my opinion if you give someone a card they can see before opening it, the friendship is rather tenuous! However, the biggest test was the design on the card. Father Christmases, humorous, decorated trees, robins, doves and ice-skating penguins are fine, but if you get one with bells, baubles, candles, or those old-fashioned carriages rushing through a snowy scene, you know this person intently dislikes you. To take it a step further, if there is any trace of that horrible cheap crusty glitter on the card, you can be sure they positively hate you! Anyway, annoying as it was then, it's worked out very handy to have them now. (*Pulls cracker with himself, puts on hat, tells joke and plays with gift*)

Since I left the old firm things have been a bit thin on the cards front. Bit thin on the everything front – friends, visitors, going out, hair! I haven't really got anything to show from before three years ago, before Kate and I split, well before Kate walked out: 21st of October 1997, at approximately a quarter past six. I thought everything was fine, but I hadn't reckoned on Alasdair. (*Blows raspberry*) Alasdair, the hunky chunky surveyor from East Dulwich. . . . Swept her off her feet. . . . Twelve years together, gone – pooff, a mere trifle. I put a manly face on it. (*Mimic a cool dude*) 'Yeah babe, you're probably right: time to move on. You know what they say – if you love someone set them free. If they come back again then in the end it was meant to be.' But I didn't want to let her go free. I wanted her exclusively for myself. I wanted to give myself exclusively to her, no one else. It wasn't selfish, it was absolute love, bordering on obsession. We were never apart. Here's her picture, and oh, I'll play you our song. It's an absolute classic. (*Finds tape then plays Nat King Cole's 'Unforgettable'. He looks through photo album singing along. Pours large drink*)

We didn't keep any Christmas cards in the years we were together. We used to cut out the pictures with pinking shears and donate them to Save the Dolphins to sell the following year as gift tags. I mean, who needs to feel popular and loved by friends when you have each other? It was complete, perfect, unforgettable. (*Picks up nut crackers*) Hello Alasdair, it's lovely to meet you. (*Throws down crackers*) Oh, when is that Bond movie going to start? Two hours and 11 minutes precisely.

Have you ever tried a Christmas on your own? Oh, they are unforgettable. Ah! (*Sings*) Unforgettable. . . . You don't know what you're missing; we're just about to kick into a big party here. (*He talks to a half-eaten chicken*) Hey chick, wanna dance? Ooh beautiful bit of breast on you. I think you've been drinking though; you look half gone! Half gone, get it? Boom, boom. . . . Come on, chick, you know you want me. (*He picks up by legs and dances around singing 'Unforgettable'*) It's funny how Christmas is a kind of magnifier of how you feel. If you're a happy family it makes you happier; if you're sad it gets you really sad; if you're generous you have a huge spend; if you're tight it makes you feel mega stingy . . . and, if you're lonely, well, you can guess. How can I explain it? Everything about Christmas, the TV shows, the gifts, the colours, the decorations, the happy songs, the cards, huh . . . they all seem to scream out, 'YOU ARE SAD AND LONELY!' When it's not Christmas it's bearable. Christ born in a stable of a virgin – was it to save me or torment me? Ah well, I suppose it's my own fault. I didn't have to be on my own. I mean, the phone is two way: I could have gone with Mum and Dad over to their friends, the Butlers. There's always a big crowd there. They would have welcomed me, but they're all so flipping happy. Mrs Butler gives everyone a present, even if it is only a 39p talcum powder from Superdrug . . . and of course, they play all the classic Christmas games. (*Acts out Charades*) Oh TV . . . two words . . . hat, wave . . . Queen . . . coronation . . . *CORONATION STREET*! And Mrs Butler's *pièce de résistance*, can you remember the 20 items on the tray under the tea cloth? Then after a tea consisting of cheese footballs, dates, Twiglets and assorted sliced meats, they'll all sit round the TV and watch the Christmas special of *One Foot in the Grave*. Oh please God I don't end up like Victor Meldrew: 'I don't *believe* it!!' I was going to phone Mum about going this year, but I don't know – a 37-year-old man going to a Christmas do with his mum and dad. SADDO!! I mean, it's not pride, well, yeah I suppose it is pride really. I could've gone to see Rob in Morecambe. I nearly picked up the phone for that one. 'Hey Rob, how about a visitor for Christmas?' 'Yeah, great mate. Anytime; it gets boring up here between shows. We could hit some bars, find some fillies eh! I'll flash my Equity card about, let them all know I'm an actor. They'll be falling at our feet.' It could have been good fun I admit, but they're doing three shows a day, for goodness' sake. By the time he's got out of his camel's rear-end costume, we'll only have half an hour before he's back on again – and the accommodation, well you think this is bad? A flea-infested damp dump in a Morecambe guest house, with the Wicked Witch of the West as your landlady is not my ideal digs. No, give me Mary Poppins and a Pot Noodle any day.

I suppose that brings me back to Kate. I don't think I told you the rest of the Alasdair saga. You're probably thinking to yourself, while I sit here alone, Kate and Alasdair in contrast are having a happy family Christmas with their 2.4 children and two thirds of a dog. (*Buzzer noise*) WRONG! They didn't have a happy ending. No, after a year Alasdair the stud gave Kate a taste of her own medicine. He left her for a younger more attractive model. I don't know if he's still with her – probably changed a couple of times since. Blokes like him always do. But Kate, Kate's on her own. I hear she lives alone in a flat in Hove, depressed and lonely. Similar to me really, except she's more a *Sound of Music* kinda girl! I know what you're all saying: call her up. I've thought about it. Believe me, every day I think about it, but if she wants me, she can get in touch. I'm ready, I think I'm ready. (*The phone rings, JOHN ignores it*)

That phone you might have heard, it's not actually my phone. It's actually my imagination. Often I hear it ring. I imagine answering it to talk to all manner of interesting people, to Kate. We talk about the old times, the mistakes, the lessons. We begin to build a future together, without loneliness, only happiness. (*Phone rings again*) 'But how do you know it's not your phone ringing?' I hear you say. Because my phone is broken. (*He picks up phone and we can see it is disconnected*) And anyway, I know because even when it worked, it never rang. (*He throws phone down and pours another drink*)

I have built the ultimate defence mechanism for my emotions. No one visits, no one calls. I visit no one, I call no one. Let nobody near you, protect your territory, then nobody can hurt you . . . da na na. . . . A life without hurt – it's as easy as that. But the price is high. Nobody can hurt you, but nobody can love you. That's the deal. Did you know that statistics prove that the suicide rate at Christmas increases? I wonder why. Oh don't panic, I've done this before on numerous occasions, but what have I got to live for? A James Bond film and a leftover chicken sandwich. (*He sings 'Unforgettable' to himself and bursts out crying*) Kate . . . KATE . . . KATE!! (*'Unforgettable' plays as lights fade to blackout*)

TEACHING POINT

The best way to help the lonely is to befriend them.

BIBLE REFERENCE

Proverbs 18:24

Up on the Roof

Better to live on a corner of the roof than share a house with a quarrelsome wife.

INTRODUCTION

I have based this sketch on a literal translation of Proverbs 25:24, in my opinion the verse in the Bible which most naturally lends itself to comedy. Designed for laughs, the sketch can easily stand on its own. It also brings up issues relating to bitter quarrels and rocky relationships. The actor playing Harold is laid back and has a hint of sarcasm, and Agnes is a dreadful hag, somewhat in the tradition of a pantomime dame.

Characters: HAROLD, PETER, AGNES.

HAROLD is sitting on the corner of a roof, happily reading. PETER enters and stops to look up at him. There is a confused pause before he speaks.

PETER: Hello.

HAROLD: (*Continues reading*) Hello.

PETER: All right up there are you?

HAROLD: Yes, thank you, on top of the world.

PETER: Only, it seems a bit strange, you sittin' there, on the corner of a roof.

HAROLD: Mmm?

PETER: I was just saying, it's odd you being up on the roof. You're not thinking of doing anything . . . well, anything silly?

HAROLD: (*Confused*) Anything silly?

PETER: Like jumping.

HAROLD: Jumping? From this height? Are you mad?

PETER: Well, I was just worried that . . .

HAROLD: Oh, I see! You were worried I was thinking of. . . . (*Mimes diving*)

PETER: Precisely.

HAROLD: No no no no no! Fret not. (*He continues reading*)

PETER: (*Short pause*) So, if you don't mind me asking, why are you up there?

HAROLD: Why am I on my roof?

PETER: Yes.

HAROLD: Well, I live here.

PETER: I beg your pardon?

HAROLD: I live here, up on the roof. (*Sings a line from 'Up on the Roof'*)

PETER: (*Shocked*) You live on your roof?! For pity's sake, why?

HAROLD: Aha. . . . My wife.

PETER: Your wife?

HAROLD: Yes, the good old trouble and strife, the ball and chain, the better half, 'er indoors!

PETER   So what you're saying is your wife makes you live on the roof?

HAROLD: She didn't make me, I chose to. And you would too if you'd married her.

PETER: She can't be that bad, surely?

HAROLD: Oh dear, oh dear. You've obviously not met her. She makes Nora Batty look like Mother Teresa.

PETER: That bad, eh?

HAROLD: Worse.

PETER: So how long have you been married to her?

HAROLD: Oooh. Must be 17 years now.

PETER: And how long have you lived up there?

HAROLD: (*Pause to think*) Sixteen-and-a-half years.

PETER: It only lasted six months!

HAROLD: Listen pal, six months with the original fire-breathing dragon and her doolally mother would have tried the patience of Job.

PETER: Well, if she's that bad, why on earth did you marry her?

HAROLD: Well, she was as nice as pie to start off with, yes. We had our few months of bliss. . . . Then, she got that ring on her finger, and it all started going downhill. . . . You married?

PETER: Yeah.

HAROLD: How long?

PETER: Three months.

HAROLD: (*Sharp intake of breath*) Honeymoon period that, mate. I'd make the most of it if I were you. Have you started to notice any little changes yet?

PETER: (*Pause*) Now you come to mention it, she's not so keen on bringing me breakfast in bed any more.

HAROLD: Ahhh! You see, that's the first thing to go. Call me a cynic but, if you ask me, it's the beginning of the end for you.

PETER: That may be true, but I just can't imagine things being so bad that you're driven to live on a roof for sixteen-and-a-half years!

HAROLD: How innocent and naïve you are . . .

AGNES: (*Off stage*) HAROLD!!

HAROLD: Oh blimey, here we go.

PETER: Is this her?

HAROLD: Yep, this is my adorable Agnes. Get the fire extinguishers ready and stand back at a safe distance.

AGNES: (*Storms on*) Harold Winterbottom, I want words with you.

HAROLD: (*Sarcastically over the top*) Ah Agnes, light of my
miserable life. What can I do for you?

AGNES: How many times have I told you, if you're gonna
live on that confounded roof, DON'T TIDDLE
DOWN THE CHIMNEY!!

HAROLD: Not guilty, my cream peach. I think you'll find
that's your incontinent mother marking out her territory.

AGNES: Ohhhhh! Don't you blame my mother.

HAROLD: Oh just admit it, Agnes, she's totally senile and
gets the fireplace mixed up with the karzy – it's an
easy mistake to make.

HAROLD: How dare you speak about my mother like that!
She's the most wonderful person that ever walked
God's earth. Why oh why didn't I listen to her 17
years ago? She said you'd turn out no good. She
always thought you were a lily-livered mamby
pamby with the brains of a lollipop, and by gum
she was right! (*AGNES spots PETER, stares and
addresses him viciously*) What do you want?

PETER: (*Jumpy*) Oh, nothing.

AGNES: Who are you, then?

PETER: Oh . . . ah . . . um . . . my, my name is Peter. It's a
pleasure to meet you.

AGNES: Why are you here?

PETER: I was just passing the day chatting with your husband.

AGNES: Poor you! I should steer clear of him if I were you
– you might pick up his rudeness and bad habits.

HAROLD: Well, I'm sure after chatting with you he'll have
the milk of human kindness pumping through his
veins, my precious cutesie pie.

AGNES: Don't you cutesie pie me, Mr smarty pants. You're

not off the hook. If it wasn't for my acute case of vertigo I'd be up there to sort you out.

HAROLD: Precisely the reason I moved up here in the first place.

AGNES: (*To PETER*) See what I mean? He's a rude, selfish, ignorant warthog. (*Upset*) I threw the prime years of my life away on him. Look at me now, a woman spurned. My mother warned me; she said he'd turn out no good. He's a lily-livered mamby pamby with the brains of a lollipop, and by gum she was right! (*HAROLD mimes some of this speech which has obviously become very familiar*) I should've listened to her, but in my youth I was overcome by animal attraction. Little did I know that the animal would turn out to be a big fat greasy heffalump. (*To HAROLD*) And you, Mr king of his stupid castle, you can forget about any dinner tonight – I'm giving yours to the dog!

HAROLD: Oh, poor old Spot, what's he done to deserve that? I wouldn't trust the salad dressing anyway, not with your mother on the loose!

AGNES: Oh you lowlife, woollybacked, lunkheaded, bonebrained, poopbagged, toeraggedy, fuddy-duddy deadbeat! All I can say to you is, I HOPE IT RAINS. Mother, where are you? MOTHER!! (*Agnes exits*)

HAROLD: (*Stunned pause*) Well, I sure know how to pick 'em! Anyway Peter, good to meet you. You must pop by again some time.

PETER: (*Deep in thought*) Mmmm.

HAROLD: I said, you must pop by again some time.

PETER: Yes, I will. I was just wondering. . . .

HAROLD: What?

PETER: Well, just in case. Is there room up there for two?
           (*HAROLD smiles as lights fade to blackout*)

TEACHING POINT

Quarrels are rarely harmless, and often lead to bitter feuds.

BIBLE REFERENCE

Proverbs 25:24

The Vanishing Princess

Reckless words pierce like a sword, but the tongue of the wise brings healing.

INTRODUCTION

Never has the Bible been more relevant than when it speaks of the power we can unleash by simply using the tongue. I wanted this sketch to have at its centre the cruel, life-threatening illness, anorexia. I do not claim to be an expert on this subject, and I know there can be numerous reasons for an individual to suffer from anorexia, but in this piece the trigger is negative use of the tongue. A possible solution introduced at the end of the sketch is the positive use of the tongue. The piece is designed to be hard hitting and thought provoking, and will need a strong female actor to play Paula. Little is required in the way of props and scenery, and the monologue will serve well on its own or with teaching on uses of the tongue.

Character: PAULA.

Lights come up on PAULA, seated centre stage. She addresses the audience directly.

PAULA: I'm no expert, but if you ask me it all started for her back at school, primary school even. She was never part of the in-crowd – you know, that snooty group of girls that parade around like the Pink Ladies in *Grease*, gaggles of boys agog, following their every move. No, she was never one of them, but she had a nice little group of friends, you know, just . . . well, nice. Anyway, the other kids decided to nickname her Porky Pig. (*Attempts funny voice*) P P P Porky P P P Pig! Now I know as a mother I'm probably somewhat biased, but really, with any stretch of the imagination you couldn't call her fat or porky. Don't get me wrong, she wasn't skinny then. No, just, well, you know, normal. But you know kids, they never let up, do they? So Porky Pig it remained. We knew it upset her a bit, but Richard and I used to make light of it. 'Oh just ignore them,' we would say. 'If they see it doesn't bother you, they'll soon get bored and leave you alone.' But that was the problem: it did bother her, and kids have got an uncanny ability to know just when they're hitting the spot. It continued all through primary school. We didn't particularly know at the time. I mean, how could we? She never said anything. Looking back now, though, I can see the effect. As a toddler she had so much joy: I can picture her beaming smile now, her cute little pigtails, her laughing and skipping. She was the life and soul of the party . . . but slowly that all disappeared. She became a loner, so introverted; it was all Richard could do to get her to smile. A couple of years before, he would play with her and she would instantly fall into wild hysterics – it was a sight to behold. Neither of us could understand what was happening, what was happening to our little princess.

I think part of her was relieved to be leaving primary school, which she of course saw as a place of daily torture; but the other part was filled with dread at moving up to grown-up school. I dropped her off on the first morning – ashen-faced she was. I didn't think too much of it. 'Of course she's nervous,' I thought. 'Everybody is, on their first day at a new school.' At home things remained the same: she was quiet, moody. But at school, as we were to find out later, things had taken a cruel turn. The Porky Pig nickname had obviously run its course – it was probably seen as being a bit babyish for her youthful tormentors. I suppose it could even have been seen by some as a term of affection. The same mistake could not be made of her new epithet. Fat cow, fat cow. FAT COW! (*Pause*) What can drive one human being to call another human being such a terrible thing? Week in, week out, day after day, hour after hour: 'FAT COW, FAT COW, FAT COW!!' We knew nothing about it – if we had, Richard and I would have been straight up to the school to see the head. I could see she was unhappy, though. I should have forced her to tell me why, gone up to see her teachers anyway, but you don't, do you? You just let it go on and on and on.

It was in her first year at senior school that she started on the dieting. At first I thought it was just a fad – you know, one of these things teenagers go through, nothing to worry about. But as the weeks and months went on it got progressively more serious, to the point where she was hardly eating anything at all. Dry toast, a few vegetables. A bit of fruit if you were lucky. It all had the desired effect, though: the weight literally fell off her, stone after stone after stone. Richard hadn't got a clue what was going on. 'Ah, get a few burgers and fry-ups down her – she'll be as good as gold.' It's not that he didn't care – he just didn't understand. She slowly became this walking skeleton, her bones visible – that's on the rare occasion they weren't covered in huge baggy jumpers. We started going through the endless rounds of doctors, dieticians and specialists, but I don't know if they do any good. Richard never speaks about it, typical man keeping it all huddled in, but I know from time to time he cries. On his own in the bedroom. I've heard him. I don't go in though; he needs to keep his steel exterior intact. But I know it breaks his heart to see his little princess vanishing.

I've been doing a bit of research. I was never much of a scholar, I admit, but it's been really interesting. Lots of stuff about eating disorders, anorexia, bulimia, and even psychology for beginners. I thought I had to do something, I just felt so helpless. My daughter vanishing before my eyes, and me not knowing what to do. Of course these books say how all the professional help can work, but they also say that so many victims overcome their problem by the support and love of family and friends. Now I don't understand all that Freud and Jung stuff – it's much too brainy for me. But I've got this belief that all the lies she was told – the Porky Pig, the fat cow, the waste of space – that I have the power to drown all this out, by telling her over and over the truth as it is, as I see it. (*PAULA starts to cry*) That she's fearfully and wonderfully made. That she is beautiful. That she is precious. That she is worth so much and has so much to live for. Can't she see that? Please, let her see that. (*Pause to try and compose herself*) Oh God, dear God, I don't want much, maybe I don't deserve much, but please don't take my child from me. I can weather a storm like anyone else, but I don't think I can cope if I have to outlive my child, my only child, my princess. . . . (*PAULA sobs; soft music drowns her crying. Lights fade to blackout*)

TEACHING POINT

Be careful what you say to people, even in jest – it can have long-lasting effects.

BIBLE REFERENCE

Proverbs 12:18

Vince the Lad

A generous man will himself be blessed, for he shares his food with the poor.

INTRODUCTION

I originally wrote this monologue to perform at a presentation highlighting issues surrounding Third World need. Vince is a typical 19-year-old lad: into football, booze and girls. As such he may seem a strange choice of character to highlight Third World poverty, but it is because he is so unlikely that he challenges us all – although we may care about poverty, do we care enough actually to do anything about it?

Proverbs reflects the whole of the Bible in what it has to say about our responsibility to help the poor, and how if we do help, we will be richly blessed. The piece should be loud and punchy, and is best played with a strong cockney accent. Dressing up in a Ben Sherman shirt, baggy jeans and Doc Marten boots will also work well.

Character: VINCE.

VINCE is waiting for his girlfriend to get ready for their evening out. As he does so he addresses the audience. The sketch opens with loud music, and as lights go up VINCE is standing centre stage with his back to the audience. When the music stops, he starts.

VINCE: (*Shouting upstairs*) STONE THE CROWS! GET A SHIFT ON, SANDRA!! (*To audience*) I dunno about all this political correctness lark that's going round at the moment, but I tell ya, there's nothing I like more than standing on the top of my ladder, giving my window a good chamois, looking down at the lovely ladies and calling out in my best Queen's English, 'OI OI OI, HOWZABOUT IT THEN, DARLING, EH EH EH!' (*In typical laddish fashion he adjusts his underwear*) Ooh 'scuse me while I make a quick adjustment. That's better. Don't get me wrong, I don't think them right-wing feminists are a big fan, but most of the girls who walk down the Islington High Street absolutely love it! For instance, take Sandra, my new bird. Fell prey to my charms a few months back. Now boys, listen and learn. I chatted it up one lunchtime when I was doing the windows of the building society she works at, right. That same evening I treated her to an à la carte doner kebab, invited her back to my gaff, stuck me Greatest Hits of Madness CD on and knocked her sideways no problem. I dunno how I manage it – I must be a natural or summink! . . . (*Shouts upstairs*) SANDRA!!

Anyway, my boys I hang out with – the Highbury Mafia they call us – a right bunch of desperadoes, they couldn't pull a bird if she had one arm and a winch! (*Impersonates his mates*) 'Vince,' they say. 'Vince, how do you do it with all the birds, mate?' 'I dunno,' I say. 'I think the phrase you're looking for is "animal magnetism"!' The only reason why such a suave, sophisticated guy like me hangs out with this bunch of yobbish losers is for our Saturday afternoon soirées at Highbury Stadium. We all pile in the North stand, sink a few pints, have a bit of a laugh, kick a few away-supporters' heads in, and if there's time we even watch a bit of football. Can't be bad. I tell ya, there's nothing quite like the sound of a Doc Marten boot connecting with the head of a Man United supporter, followed by the ringing tones of (*Chants*) 'YOU'RE GOING HOME IN A LONDON AMBULANCE!!' You might think it all sounds a bit violent, but it's only a bit of a laugh, innit! Blimey, where's it got to? (*Shouts upstairs*) SANDRA!!

She's up there at the mo, tarting herself up with her best mate Vicky. Vicky, who wears skirts the width of a bit of dental floss, applies her make-up with a trowel, and managed to just about scrape one GCSE in needlework! What we lads call easy prey, if you know what I mean. Still, I can't complain about my Sandra – she's a good girl, brought me a lovely present this afternoon. A new Ben Sherman shirt and a bottle of Paco Rabanne. Once I've got that lot on I'll be sorted. She said to me the other day (*Impersonates Sandra*) 'Ooh Vince, do you know why I love you so much?' Well, I would of answered, but it could have been one of a thousand things, so I let her go on. (*Continues impression*) 'I love you 'cos you're such a nineties man!' Now, I wouldn't have thought of that, but give it a bit of credit – she's quite right, 'cos I am in touch with my more caring and feminine side. Example: last Friday, I treated her to a slap-up fish and chip supper. Now, I only got about halfway through mine 'cos my guts were giving me jip – my own fault, I'd had six pints and a dodgy curry the night before. Anyway, Miss Sarky Moo says, 'Ooh, what a waste! There's millions starving in Africa who'd give their right arm for that.' So without thinking, and in hindsight rather stupidly, I chucked it at her and said, 'Well, send it to 'em then!' Now, as soon as I said it I realised how daft it sounded, 'cos it's not really practical to shove a half-eaten tray of haddock, chips and mushy peas into a Jiffy bag and send it to Africa. For a start who would you send it to? Genghis Khan? Muppetma Gandhi?

Winston Mandela? So as a compromise I took it home,
bunged it in the blender and served it up as a treat for my
cute pit bull called Sultan. He loved it. But back to my caring and feminine side. You see the whole thing's been playing on my mind ever since. I mean, think about it: all the
spare food that's kicking around that nobody wants or
needs – why can't they be sent it? Not in dribs and drabs in
Jiffy bags, but you know, as a big job lot, like. I suppose
it's all got to do with them political sanitations, but to be
frank, I don't suppose a starving family in Africa gives two
hoots about a couple of prattish bureaucrats arguing over
the export price of bananas! Still, that's the world for you,
innit? What can you do? Well, there's nothing you can do,
is there? (*Shouts upstairs*) SANDRA!! (*VINCE freezes in
position with back to audience. Blackout*)

TEACHING POINT

Do we make a real effort to help the poor and needy of the
world, or do we resign ourselves and say, 'There's nothing
you can do'?

BIBLE REFERENCE

Proverbs 22:9

Subject Index

Scripture Index

Proverbs

50 Sketches About Jesus

by David Burt

Picture the scene: Jesus preaching at Wembley
Stadium; a paparazzi photographer in Bethlehem;
Mary cooking spaghetti hoops on toast; the wise men
shopping in Harrods.

Strange? Maybe. Funny? Certainly. But every sketch
highlights a truth about Jesus of Nazareth that is
relevant to life today.

There's something here for all levels of expertise, and
all ages. Fully indexed by themes, occasions and Bible
references, this is an ideal resource for churches and
other groups who wish to communicate old truths in
fresh ways.